FROM POST OFFICE TO ART CENTER

From Post Office to Art Center

A NASHVILLE LANDMARK IN TRANSITION

Foreword by Chase W. Rynd

Text by Christine Kreyling
with Keel Hunt and the Staff of the Frist Center for the Visual Arts

FRIST CENTER FOR THE VISUAL ARTS
Nashville, Tennessee

FRIST

CENTER FOR THE VISUAL ARTS

This book is published in conjunction with the exhibition "From Post Office to Art Center: A Nashville Landmark in Transition," April 8, 2001– February 24, 2002, organized by the Frist Center for the Visual Arts and presented by AmSouth.

Publication of this book was made possible in part by

The Frist Foundation

AmSouth

Library of Congress Control Number: 2001 131053
ISBN: 0-9706979-2-9 (cloth)
ISBN: 0-9706979-3-7 (paper)
ISBN: 0-9706979-6-1 (3-volume set, cloth)
ISBN: 0-9706979-7-X (3-volume set, paper)

Cover: Seab A. Tuck III, *Frist Center for the Visual Arts*. Based on a photograph of the Marr & Holman presentation drawing, *Tennessean* archives. Graphite on paper; 13¾ × 24 in. Frist Center for the Visual Arts.

Frontispiece: Detail, Phil Ponder (American, b. 1933), *Frist Center for the Visual Arts*, 1999. Color lithograph; 12½ × 16 in.

Endpapers: Marr & Holman, Architects, *Entrance Vestibule and Lobby Details, Nashville Post Office*. Ink on linen; 31 × 39 in. Metropolitan Development and Housing Agency, on deposit with the Frist Center for the Visual Arts.

Designed by Susan E. Kelly
Copyedited by Fronia W. Simpson
Produced by Marquand Books, Inc., Seattle
    www.marquand.com
Printed by C&C Offset Printing Co., Ltd., Hong Kong

CONTENTS

SPONSOR'S STATEMENT

AmSouth

When needs are understood, needs can be met.
When needs are met, relationships are built
and grow stronger.

These opening sentences from AmSouth's Mission Statement guide our company and our employees every day. Understand Needs. Meet Needs. Build Relationships. It is the way we do business at AmSouth, but it is also a philosophy that describes our commitment to community. In addition, this philosophy is shared by the leaders who built the Frist Center for the Visual Arts.

Throughout the Southeast, the nation, and beyond, AmSouth employees work diligently to meet the financial needs of their customers. But they do much more. In every AmSouth market, lives are improved and communities are enriched through the efforts of our valued employees.

On behalf of our employees, AmSouth is proud to join in the historic opening of the Frist Center for the Visual Arts with our sponsorship of the Center's inaugural exhibitions.

FOREWORD

The opportunity to participate in the creation of a significant new visual arts organization does not present itself very often. Also infrequent is the opportunity to become immersed in a high-profile historic preservation project. The moment when both such opportunities converge in a singular and remarkable scheme is extremely rare. The founding of the Frist Center for the Visual Arts represents just such a moment, for the Frist Center anticipates the future as a vital new arts institution while it honors the past by conserving Nashville's former main post office building.

We must credit the community-wide forces behind the establishment of the Frist Center for their wise course of action. By locating the Center in the post office, the region receives two benefits simultaneously: a recycled historic building ready to serve us anew and a downtown visual arts institution designed to present the history of art of all eras and cultures.

Each of us on the staff of the Frist Center was attracted to the possibilities associated with a "start-up" organization. Beginning with a fresh, clean slate, we were handed the opportunity to invent the institution and our roles within it. By devising innovative programs and collaborating with many other organizations in Nashville, we have been shaping our own signature within the community. This has been an inspiring, often overwhelming, frequently fun, sometimes exhausting, and ultimately rewarding process for all of us. What most of us did not anticipate was how compelling and intriguing it would be to work also on the building renovation with Tuck Hinton Architects and the rest of our project colleagues. This—a chance to contribute to the physical shape of our new home—was a bonus, and it made our jobs both more interesting and more complicated.

On that note, it is imperative that the founding staff of the Frist Center be applauded. There is no question that each person faced—at one point or another—significant challenges, impossible deadlines, tedious tasks, serious frustrations, and some disappointments. And each person responded with professional aplomb as we strove to achieve our shared goal. As a group, we have supported one another's efforts and cheered each other's accomplishments. And we have laughed, a lot. I thank all Frist Center staff members for their commitment to this project, for their persistence, for their seriousness of purpose, and for their humor. The generous spirit of the Frist Center is perfectly embodied in this tremendous group of people.

The members of the Board of Trustees of the Frist Center also deserve the highest compliments for their dedication to this project. The Board has been thoroughly engaged in the planning and development of the organization and has consistently provided the staff with wise counsel and encouragement. Their enthusiasm for the project, blended with their shared concern for Nashville's well-being, has charged the staff with the highest level of energy. Of particular note are the contributions of Dr. Thomas F. Frist, Jr., and Kenneth L. Roberts, Chairman and President of the Board of Trustees, respectively. It is widely acknowledged that were it not for their total belief in a vision, their perseverance, and their genuine affection for this community, the Frist Center for the Visual Arts would never have materialized. Both men must be acknowledged for their leadership and altruism.

Recognizing the widespread interest in the old main post office building, the Frist Center staff decided early on to produce an exhibition and publication addressing its history—from the original construction through its transformation into an art center. As the guest curator selected to organize this exhibition and craft the primary essay, Christine Kreyling has done an outstanding job. Her research produced fascinating visual and anecdotal material, while her keen sense of history and engaging descriptive style have brought the building's story to life. I thank her for taking on such a formidable task and delivering such good results.

There are a number of other people who contributed a great deal to this exhibition and book. Candace J. Adelson, Exhibitions Curator, worked tirelessly overseeing the logistics of the project. Doug Fisher, Exhibitions Designer, collaborated with Mrs. Kreyling to develop the look and layout of the exhibition. Seab A. Tuck III, principal with Tuck Hinton Architects, provided invaluable information and insights about the building, while his colleagues, Mary Roskilly and Amanda Lightman-Jones, assisted with our research. Carl Munkel from Gresham, Smith and Partners was the construction Program Manager and was always available to provide access to the building and direct us to appropriate contacts. Of course we are very grateful to the lenders of objects to the exhibition: Mr. W. Ridley Wills II and Tuck Hinton Architects. And we are equally appreciative of the efforts on our behalf by those colleagues who assisted with research: Ken Fieth and John Lancaster of Metro Archives; Mary Glenn Hearne and Carol Kaplan of the Nashville Room, Nashville Public Library; Susan Gordon and Julia Rather of the Tennessee State Library & Archives; Jim Hoobler and Steve Cox of the Tennessee State Museum; Ann Roberts and her staff at the Metro Historical Commission; Meg Ausman of the U.S. Postal Service; David Pfeiffer at the National Archives; James Bruns at the U.S. Postal Museum; Richard Cote at the Treasury Department; Pat Emery from the Gulch Group; and Mike Hoyal of the Tennessee State Division of Archaeology. Keel Hunt, our resident institutional historian and government relations guide, provided important information and counsel in equal measure. Our own Adelaide Vienneau, Community Outreach Manager, did a great job organizing a series of oral history sessions that added a wonderful personal context to our research. Through her efforts, Christine Kreyling was able to document the comments of Nelson Andrews, Charles J. Elder, Herbert Fox, Juanita Threalkill Johnson, and Marvin Runyon—all of which are recorded in this volume. Administrative Assistants Carol Fisher and Wallace Joiner, as well as interns Greg Phillipy and Caroline Timmerman, provided critical assistance to both Christine Kreyling and Candace Adelson. We thank Susan E. Kelly and Marquand Books, Inc., for the superb design of this publication and Fronia W. Simpson for her invaluable copyediting.

The exhibition and catalogue would not have been possible without the assistance of two significant partners. AmSouth is the exclusive sponsor of our inaugural exhibitions, and its support contributed to the success of this project. And, of course, none of this would have been feasible without the commitment and generosity of The Frist Foundation.

April 8, 2001, is an important milestone for the old main post office building, marking its transformation into a visual arts center. This book and the accompanying exhibition serve to document for future generations this most historic moment. All of us associated with the Frist Center for the Visual Arts are honored to be a part of this legacy.

Chase W. Rynd
Executive Director and CEO

► Fig. 1. *The Team That Built the Center*, October 2000. On Halloween eve, as construction headed down the home stretch, some of those involved in the development of the Frist Center visited the building and gathered on the grand stairway for a photograph.

BEHIND THE FRIST CENTER FOR THE VISUAL ARTS

COLLECTORS COUNCIL

Marlene Hays
Spencer Hays
Walter G. Knestrick
Judith O. Liff
Donnie Nichols
Chase W. Rynd
Walter Schatz
W. Lucas Simons
Mrs. David Steine
Hope Stringer
Howard Stringer

COUNCIL OF PARTNER INSTITUTIONS

Belle Meade Plantation
Donna Russell, Suzanne Iler

Belmont Mansion
Mark Brown

Cheekwood—Tennessee Botanical Gardens and Museum of Art
Jane Jerry and John Wetenhall

Country Music Foundation
Kyle Young

Fisk University and Fisk University Galleries
George Neely and Opal Baker

Frist Center for the Visual Arts
Walter G. Knestrick and
    Chase W. Rynd

The Hermitage: Home of Andrew Jackson
Jim Vaughan, Marcia Mullin

Nashville Public Library
Donna Nicely

The Parthenon
Wesley Paine

Tennessee State Museum
Lois Riggins-Ezell

Vanderbilt University and Vanderbilt University Fine Arts Gallery
E. F. Infante, Ph.D., John H. Venable,
    Ph.D., and Joseph S. Mella

ARTISTS COUNCIL

Jane Braddock
Michael Cooper
Kathryn Dettwiller
Tony Gerber
Nancy C. Hall
Bettye Harwell
Walter G. Knestrick
Andrée LeQuire
Michael J. McBride
Susan Mulcahy
Marilyn Murphy
Craig Nutt
Bruce Peebles
Phil Ponder
Jairo Prado
Greg Ridley
Vando L. Rogers, Jr.
Chase W. Rynd
Jacqueline Saporiti
Yoné Sinor
Joe Sorci
Terry Thacker
James R. Threalkill
Robert M. Vantrease

FRIST CENTER FOR THE VISUAL ARTS STAFF

Candace J. Adelson, Ph.D.
Marta Allen
David Bassett
Emily Bond
Anne Calton
Nancy Cason, Ph.D.
Michael Christiano
Lisa Davis
Kathy Demonbreun
Janice Dockery
Kim Carpenter Drake
Ernest Duncan
Susie Elder
Jon Emmitt
Carol Fisher
Amie Geremia
Sone-Seráe Harper

Anne Henderson
Suzy Herron
Erin M. Hinton
Sheri Horn
Amy James
Roxanne Johnson
S. Wallace Joiner
Steve Kirby
Carol Klahn
Adriana Larios
Cheryl Neely
Andy Peterson
Ellen Jones Pryor
Kecia Ray, Ed.D.
David Rice
Chase W. Rynd
Mark W. Scala
Elizabeth A. Smith
S. Ramsey Stringham
Stephanie Strong
Lauren Thompson
Amy Verheide
Adelaide Vienneau
Patrick Williams
Opal Wilson

NASHVILLE'S AGENDA ACTION TEAM ON THE ARTS

Jack O. Bovender, Jr.
Steve Buchanan
Sigourney Cheek
Andrea Conte
James H. Fyke
Kevin Grogan
Sherry Winn Howell
Keel Hunt
Martha R. Ingram
Bill Ivey
Ruth Johnson
Judith O. Liff
Marilyn Murphy
Dianne Neal
Henry Ponder, Ph.D.
Kenneth L. Roberts
Nancy Saturn

Carroll Shanks
W. Lucas Simons
Bennett Tarleton
James R. Threalkill
Tom Turk
William M. Wilson

THE STRATEGY GROUP

Keel Hunt
Elizabeth Fielding

LEGAL COUNSEL

Wyatt, Tarrant & Combs, LLP

LORD CULTURAL RESOURCES PLANNING & MANAGEMENT INC.

Murray Frost
Lia Gordon
Barry Lord
Gail Lord
Heather Maximea
Margaret May
Maria Piacente
Ted Silberberg

CONSULTANTS

2B Technology, Inc.
Acoustiguide Corporation
Atkinson Public Relations
Blackbaud
Dye Van Mol & Lawrence
Faulkner Mackie & Cochran
Douglas Fisher
Gallery Systems
Jennifer Hamady
Heidrick & Struggles
Jerold Panas Linzy & Partners
Pamela Johnson Associates
S. W. Knowles & Associates
Christine Kreyling
Bill LaFevor
Manask & Associates
Marquand Books, Inc.
MCSI/Consolidated Media Systems
Openshaw Media Group

Perdue Research Group
Renaissance Technology
Rusty Russell
Fronia W. Simpson
Susy Watts
Anna Windrow & Associates
Elaine Wood

ARCHITECT, CONSTRUCTION, AND DESIGN

TUCK HINTON ARCHITECTS

Seab A. Tuck III
Mary Roskilly

GSC DESIGN-BUILD

John Morss
Carl Munkel
Jan Norris

R. C. MATHEWS CONTRACTOR

Bob Giese
Allen Guillory
Walker Mathews
Lee Randolph
Larry Rollins
Bill Smith

PARTICIPATING FIRMS

1220 Exhibits
Acousti, Inc.
Alexander Metals
American Ironware, Inc.
Axis Identification Systems
Barnett Ironworks
BellSouth
Birdwell Acoustics
Bock Construction
Susan Brady Light Design
Bulldog Excavating
BWSC
Central Business Group
Code Consultants, Inc.
The Comfort Group
Commercial Hydroseeding
Concrete Form Erectors

Construction Specifications, Inc.
Cumberland Architectural Millwork, Inc.
Curham Contracting
D & L Landscaping
D's Interiors
Dale, Inc.
Douglas Group
EMC Structural Engineers, P.C.
Fuhrman Glass Studios, Inc.
Global Supply and Service Company
HICO
Hodgson & Douglas
I. C. Thomasson Associates, Inc.
J & J Interiors
Kaswell Wood Flooring
Steven Keller & Associates
Leader Contractors
Levy Industrial Contractors
Liddle Brothers
McCampbell & Associates, AIA
McCarthy, Jones, Woodard
Manning Materials
Metro Ready Mix
Mid-South Wrecking Company, Inc.
Morley Enterprises
Music City Fire Sprinkler
Nashville Machine Company
Noise Pollution Control Company, Inc.
Ove Arup and Partners
Pan American Electric Company
Planning Design & Research
Quinn/Evans
Rackley Roofing
Renato Bertoli Marble & Tile, Inc.
Rosa Mosaic Tile
S. E. J. Cement Finishing
Scruggs, Inc.
Shelley Reisman Paine Conservation
Southern Embroidery & Logo, Inc.
Special Finishes, Inc.
Universal Solutions
Walker Parking Consultants
WASCO, Inc.
Welding Techniques, Inc.

MISSION OF THE FRIST CENTER FOR THE VISUAL ARTS

The Mission of the Frist Center for the Visual Arts is to provide a dynamic public facility for all Nashvillians that will stimulate and nourish their appreciation, understanding and creativity in the visual arts through a wide range of aesthetically significant, educational and entertaining programs for all ages;

and to open a "Window on the World" for Nashvillians and their visitors through a program of exciting and inspiring exhibitions of works of art in all media and of all historical periods from across the nation and around the globe;

achieving both aims through cooperation with all other museums, educational and related institutions and art organizations in the Nashville area and beyond, including the exhibition and interpretation to Nashvillians and visitors of works of art from public and private collections in the region;

with an emphasis on educational programming aimed at enriching the enjoyment, understanding and study of the visual arts, particularly by Nashville young people;

and with a commitment to serving all sectors of Nashville's diverse communities, both at the Center and through stimulating outreach programs developed in on-going consultation with those communities.

MANDATES OF THE FRIST CENTER FOR THE VISUAL ARTS

1. The Frist Center for the Visual Arts will serve Nashville as a major exhibition facility and as a community art center, but is not conceived as a collecting institution. It is committed to bring to Nashville exhibitions of the highest quality, both in content and in presentation and educational interpretation.

2. As a non-collecting institution, the Center relies upon loans of artwork from museums, collectors and artists and is necessarily responsible for the proper care and handling of all artwork in its custody. Therefore, the Center commits to meeting rigorous industry standards regarding climate control, security, art handling and preservation and conservation issues.

3. The Center has entered into partnership agreements with other local cultural and educational institutions that have art collections and/or programs complementary to the Center's mission. Partner institutions with collections have agreed to loan objects to the Center on a short- and long-term basis. In return, the Center commits to provide, when appropriate, research, documentation, publication and/or conservation related to the objects on loan. The Center also strives to identify and promote other collaborative opportunities with partner institutions, such as shared marketing and/or ticketing efforts, cross-appointments of guest curators, exhibition and education program linkages, transportation connections, etc.

4. The Center is committed to a policy of cooperation with and support for other arts and educational institutions in Nashville. The Center's Orientation Gallery, educational and outreach programs will be supportive of these institutions, encouraging Nashville residents and their visitors to discover, enjoy and learn from them. By graphic and electronic means, the Orientation Gallery will aim to acquaint Center visitors with the wide range of public and private resources in the visual arts of Nashville, and aid them to find their way to enjoy the full range of the city's visual arts scene.

5. The Center aims to be supportive of all Nashville arts and artists' organizations, and has formed the Artists Council as a means to achieve this goal. The Center is firmly committed to including artwork by Tennessee and regional artists on a regular basis throughout its exhibition program. The Center will offer meeting space to arts organizations at little or nominal cost. However, the Center cannot make indefinite commitments to providing exhibition space to any artists' group for annual or biennial shows.

6. The Center will seek to be a respected member of the international art community and, as such, to develop mutually constructive contacts, collaborations and exchanges with artists, scholars, critics, museums and art centers across the United States and abroad, as well as in Nashville and Tennessee.

7. Education at all levels will be a priority for the Center, with a strong commitment to working with Nashville's schools to enhance art education, teacher training, and the relevance of art to all aspects of the curriculum. All Nashville youth (18 and under) will be admitted free to the Center. The Center will help address the issue of obtaining sufficient buses for visits to the Center by securing grants and/or arranging for supplementary transportation. While the Center's primary educational focus will be on the Metropolitan Nashville public school system, the Center will also work closely with the city's numerous private, secondary and home schools and institutions of higher education. The Center will also develop programs appropriate to non-school groups of all ages.

8. The Center's outreach program will be developed in cooperation with facilities and organizations in the communities, such as libraries, community centers, civic and social organizations, the parks system and senior centers.

9. The Center's gift shop will provide merchandise with a distinctive level of quality and will include objects by Nashville and Tennessee artisans in accordance with this commitment to outstanding quality.

Fig. 2. Aubrey C. Watson (American, b. 1942), *Partners That Moved the Mails: The Nashville Post Office and the Union Station of the L & N Railroad*, 1990. Photograph; 10 × 8 in.

INTRODUCTION

We shape our buildings; thereafter they shape us.

—Winston Churchill, *Time*, September 12, 1960

A society projects its views of the world and the good life—and itself—in its public works, its architecture, and its land use planning. Design choices embody many forces, political and economic as well as cultural. Government buildings, therefore, must be understood in the context of the American experience.[1]

When the United States of America was founded, its leaders were faced with a challenge and an opportunity: the selection of an architectural imagery or style to embody, symbolize, and house a new government. Prior to the Revolutionary War, all significant buildings reflected the colonists' various national origins in Europe—Dutch along the Hudson River, English in Virginia, Anglo-Caribbean in South Carolina—inadvertent symbols of the monarchies, empires, and cultures against which the settlers rebelled. The new nation needed its own architecture.

Like the new country, an American architecture needed reason and order, stability and unity. When President George Washington spoke in his inaugural address of "a grand Columbian Federal city," he envisioned an architecture of unity that would symbolize the nation's legitimacy and its government's authority. Washington, Thomas Jefferson, and James Madison debated for years regarding the location of the capital and the buildings within it. To appease rival factions in North and South, a site for the District of Columbia was selected on the border between Maryland and Virginia.

Jefferson brought to the discussion a passion for the architecture of classical antiquity. For him, and for most of the founders, social meaning, not everyday functional activities, should determine the form of public buildings. The Greek and Roman styles were symbolically weighted with allusions to Greek democracy and the Roman republic. Classical architecture also had the right formal properties; its symmetry and hierarchy, clarity and predictability were the instruments that could tame a wilderness into rationality. For all these reasons, the two centers of the new government—the house of the executive and the house of Congress—were designed in the classical style, and Washington, D.C., became a classical capital. For the architecture of American government ever since, a classical robe has rarely gone out of fashion.

During the 1930s, there was a new wilderness to be disciplined—the economic no-man's land of the Depression. For the federal builder, some form of classicism seemed in order. The classicism of the 1934 Nashville Post Office (fig. 2), however, is not that of the U.S. Capitol, nor of the Tennessee State Capitol, for that matter. The post office is formal and symmetrical, but the massive block with its fluted pilasters is stripped, or starved, of obvious classical details. In retrospect, it was a symbolic recipe for economically lean times.

PROLOGUE: NASHVILLE'S FIRST FEDERAL BUILDING

Fig. 3. William Appleton Potter, Architect (American, 1842–1908), *The Nashville Customs House*, 1876–82. Chromolithographic postcard. Collection of W. Ridley Wills II.

The cornerstone for what was originally called Nashville's Custom House, Courthouse, and Post Office was laid by President Rutherford B. Hayes in 1877 (fig. 3). Hayes had triumphed in the 1876 election by means of a complex political deal. In return for the electoral votes of Louisiana, Hayes promised to end Reconstruction by withdrawing federal troops from the South, naming a Southerner to his Cabinet—who turned out to be Postmaster General David M. Key of Tennessee—and instigating a federal building program in the region. The Nashville Customs House—for which Congress had appropriated $377,000—was a payback on that promise.

Hayes's visit to Nashville was the first trip south of the Mason-Dixon Line by a U.S. president since the Civil War. In another first for the city, the Gothic Revival structure by William Appleton Potter, supervising architect for the Treasury Department, was Nashville's first federal office building. The limestone structure at 701 Broadway was to house the surveyor of customs, the steamboat inspector, the collector of internal revenue, and the courts, in addition to the postal service—federal functions that were primarily the responsibility of the Treasury Department.[2] The elaborate hand-carved stone ornament, the interior trim of cherry, and the solid brass hardware contributed to make this the most expensive project undertaken during Potter's short tenure as supervising architect.[3]

The Gothic style was clearly appropriate for churches, especially Episcopalian houses of worship, in the first half of the nineteenth century, when the Anglican Church was intent on emphasizing its foundations in medieval Catholicism. But Gothic crenelations and pinnacles were subsequently adapted for nonreligious purposes, such as Potter's, in part because Gothic allusions were so decidedly preindustrial.

Potter based his massive towered design for Nashville on the late Gothic town halls of northern Europe, as interpreted by English Victorian architects. A building in a style atypical of federal architecture, buttressed by Old World precedent of a nongovernmental nature, was perhaps the best costume for the consolidation of the federal presence in a city that had so recently been occupied by Union troops.

But Potter's use of the Gothic was just one example of a Victorian taste for a kaleidoscope of styles with vaguely historical allusions. (For example, the Second Empire style refers to the French Renaissance, Richardsonian Romanesque, to pre-Renaissance Europe.) Its ideology is best described as organic. The point was to celebrate the irregular shapes and textures of nature with architectural forms that are irregular and highly textured at a time when industrialism was stamping the natural world with roads and factories, right angles and rails of iron.

During the period following the Civil War, America's cities mushroomed and the Post Office Department struggled to provide them with services. And the Treasury Department, which was responsible for all buildings housing federal commerce, labored to respond to terrific pressures from congressmen to provide their districts with more federal bounty.

To defend his department against pork-barrel projects, in 1915 Treasury Secretary William McAdoo established a classification system for standard federal building types and locations. Four categories of construction were covered under this scheme, determining size, style, materials, and embellishments for a particular building. Each of the four categories was based on the total annual receipts for the particular postal system in question. A city with receipts that defined it as Class A qualified for a monumental building adorned with the finest of stones and woods and elaborate ornamental metalwork, situated on an important thoroughfare with high real estate values. A Class B post office employed less expensive stones, woods, and ornament. Class C and D post offices were made of brick, with little trim, designed in a locally traditional style—an "ordinary class of building such as any businessman would consider a reasonable investment in a small town."[4]

In the early 1930s, the Hoover administration—desperate to put builders back to work—approved the construction of a new Class B post office, rather than add to the Customs House. Nashville's new testament to federal largess was not to be in the Gothic style, which had retreated to the academic campus, nor in a full-blown classical one, nor even in the contemporary Art Deco style. The federal government hedged its bets on the modern vs. traditional debate with a style that compromised somewhere in the middle.

STREAMLINING THE POST OFFICE

When A. C. Webb, Jr., made his pastel *Irving Trust and Trinity Church, New York* in 1930 or 1931 (fig. 4),[5] he was illustrating an architectural dynamic that was visible all over the country. In the 1920s and 1930s, many architects shed the highly textured effects and historical quotations so admired by the nineteenth century in buildings such as Trinity Church in New York in favor of a more streamlined style with roots in

Fig. 4. A. C. Webb, Jr. (American, 1888–1975), *Irving Trust and Trinity Church, New York*, ca. 1930–31. Pastel and charcoal on paper; 24¹¹/₁₆ × 16³/₁₆ in. Cheekwood Museum of Art (84.14.66).

contemporary industrial design. Ornament was suppressed. Facades featured linear incisions that led the eye skyward.

These architects were ready to acknowledge the dominance of the machine in all aspects of American life and embrace, rather than reject, its aesthetics. At the American Institute of Architects' 1930 convention, the symposium on contemporary architecture was essentially a debate between the modernists and the traditionalists, between those who argued for the use of "modern construction and modern materials to the full, for architectural expression as well as practical ends" and those who presented the case for the eternal verities of historical styles.[6]

Webb was a Nashville native who exalted the skyscraper as the paragon of modern design and construction. In a series of highly romantic paintings and drawings of the early 1930s, he celebrated the exhilarating effect that the construction of modernistic commercial and government buildings was having on the skyline of Manhattan. But Webb could have captured the same transformation—albeit on a smaller scale—in his hometown, by recording the change in quarters of Nashville's downtown post office.

THE NASHVILLE POST OFFICE

CORNERSTONE OF NEW POST OFFICE LAID

—BANNER Staff Photo.
Assistant Secretary of the Treasury Lawrence W. Robert, Jr., is shown spreading the mortar beneath the huge two and a half ton cornerstone of Nashville's new million-dollar Post Office following ceremonies Saturday at the site of the new structure, Ninth Avenue and Broadway. Representaives of the Feederal Government, state and city attended, declaring the new building was symbolic of the growth of Nashville and her postal service which was established more than 130 years ago. It is a far cry from the little log hut on the south side of the Public Square—the first Post Office—to the present million-dollar structure now 20 per cent complete.

Fig. 5. *Cornerstone of New Post Office Laid.* From the *Nashville Banner,* November 5, 1933.

The post office "is to the body politic what the veins and arteries are to the natural—carrying, conveying rapidly and regularly to the remotest parts of the system correct information of the operations of the Government, and bringing back to it the wishes and the feelings of the people."

—Andrew Jackson, message to Congress, 1829, quoted in Craig et al., *The Federal Presence,* 165

When Franklin Roosevelt was inaugurated as president in March 1933, the wishes of the people were for work. One-third of the nation's workforce—13 million people—was on relief.[7] It had become clear that the Depression represented a long-term crisis; short-term emergency measures were not enough.

With the laying of the cornerstone of the Nashville Post Office on November 4, 1933, the federal government conveyed to the people that it was up to the task of crisis management (fig. 5). The best way to send that message was through the mails. Roosevelt realized, as Hoover had before him, that the federal government was most visible in every community in the form of the Post Office Department. According to the postal historian James Bruns, both presidents recognized that "the postal service's activities were the ones that touched the individual and collective lives of the local residents, the social interest of the overall community, and the business concerns of every neighborhood."[8] And post office construction could revitalize America by putting countless Americans back to work.

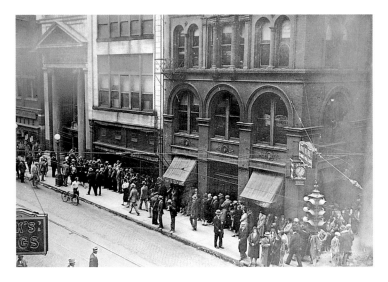

Fig. 6. *The Run on the Tennessee-Hermitage National Bank, Friday, November 14, 1930.* Photograph. Nashville Room, Nashville Public Library, Nashville, Tenn. **In response to the news that the local banking and brokerage firm of Caldwell and Company had declared insolvency on November 14, 1930, the Tennessee Hermitage National Bank suffered an all-day run. The crowd was orderly, since word had been sent down the line that all depositors would be paid in full, if they so demanded. The bank closed its doors at 2 P.M., however, with a long line of depositors still unserved.**

DEPRESSION NASHVILLE

Some of those countless Americans were Nashvillians. The city had boomed along with other urban centers in the 1920s.[9] World War I had brought the DuPont gunpowder plant, which was later converted to make rayon. Other northern textile and shoe manufacturers were drawn to Nashville's cheap labor and easy industrial policy. The budding insurance industry aggressively expanded into new markets. To promote its fortunes, National Life and Accident Insurance Company sponsored WSM—"We Shield Millions"—the radio station that would become the home of the Grand Ole Opry. The population swelled with rural-to-urban migration, as farmers fled depressed agricultural prices that had failed to float in the high tide of the Roaring Twenties.

The immediate reaction of Nashville's construction industry to the crash of October 1929 was, "It can't happen here." The *Nashville Banner* reported two months later that the city had enjoyed "a booster year of construction, and the flicker of fear that followed the stock market break . . . is being replaced by a sturdy optimism among building authorities that the 1930 volume will be substantially larger."[10] As late as October 1930, visiting officials from the Publix Theater chain proclaimed that "Nashville is one of the few cities we have seen where there is no apparent evidence of business depression."[11]

The evidence turned up, however, on November 14, 1930, when the "Wall Street of the South" went the way of the rest of the country with the bankruptcy of the local banking and brokerage firm of Caldwell and Company. In its wake, 120 banks across the South went under (fig. 6). The newspapers reported growing numbers of suicides among financially ruined businessmen. Nashville unemployment estimates shot up to 25 percent by the end of that year.

Hunger and poverty appeared on the streets of Nashville in 1931, in the form of armies of transients who camped on the banks of the Cumberland River and wandered through downtown looking for work. The middle class pawned wedding rings and family heirlooms to pay for the necessities of life. Colleges bartered for tuition, and retailers cut prices to the breaking point. Applications for help to the city's charities and public agencies rose from 2,600 in 1929 to nearly 10,000 in 1936—straining resources beyond capacity. "Relief would have to come from the government," writes Don Doyle, a historian at Vanderbilt University. "Only the federal government was up to the job."[12]

BUILDING A WAY OUT

One of the first things the Treasury Department did to provide relief for Nashville was to change its mind. Rather than add to the existing Customs House down the street, as it had previously planned, the Treasury determined to erect a new building whose sole tenant would be the post office.

There was no compelling need for more space for postal operations. A 1927 Treasury inspectors' report on Nashville's federal building notes that some departments within

FACES OF DEPRESSION NASHVILLE

In 1935 the artist Ben Shahn was on a field trip to the South and Southwest for the New Deal's Resettlement Administration, the agency charged with providing relief to America's farmers (later renamed the Farm Security Administration). The artist's assignment was to record the socioeconomic geography of some of the nation's most poverty-stricken regions and to provide himself with images for the posters and murals he had been hired to make for the agency.

During his 1935 journey, Shahn took hundreds of pictures with his Leica 35mm. Among them are a dozen of a September religious meeting in Nashville. The site was the north corner of Lower Broad, across from what was then the City Wharf on the Cumberland River. As a writer for the New Deal's Work Projects Administration recorded:

> On warm Sunday afternoons, a motley crowd of predominantly country folk gather . . . for "free-for-all preachings," a custom of twenty years standing. Anyone, Negro or white, man or woman, fundamentalist or atheist, is free to have his say. The audience, for the most part, is made up of people restlessly waiting their turn to preach. These clutch battered Bibles, which they leaf through and quote at an instant's notice. Almost without exception they have tried and discarded the standard sects. . . .
>
> Gradually the crowd extends up Broad as far as Second Avenue, and spills across First Avenue to the wharf. Preachers mount box-cars and the loading apron of the warehouse. . . . Some lure listeners by mouthing French harps or strumming banjos and guitars. Others whoop until a crowd collects. There is a constant crossfire of heckling between preachers and listeners. Furious men rush up to the preachers and shake fists, Bibles, and canes under his nose. Some ignore the preaching and draw aside to roar Scriptural quotations into each other's faces. The preaching continues until about 9 o'clock at night, when the people, satiated and subdued, begin to leave. By 10 o'clock, the corner is deserted. (Work Projects Administration for the State of Tennessee, Federal Writers Project, *The WPA Guide to Tennessee* [New York: Viking Press, 1939; reprint, Knoxville: University of Tennessee Press, 1986], 192)

Shahn's images of Nashville transcend mere reporting to explore the black and white features of a community facing hard times (figs. 7, 8).

Fig. 7. Ben Shahn (American, 1898–1969), *Religious Meeting in Nashville, Tennessee.* Photograph. U.S. Library of Congress, Prints and Photographs Division.

Fig. 8. Ben Shahn (American, 1898–1969), *Man at Religious Meeting, Nashville, Tennessee.* Photograph. U.S. Library of Congress, Prints and Photographs Division.

Hundreds of Laborers Wait on Post Office Site

—BANNER Staff Photo.
A report Tuesday morning that work was to begin on the new Post Office Building clustered the site at Ninth Avenue and Broadway with a crowd of about 1,200 men, part of which is shown above. Brick carriers, carpenters, masons, plumbers, and members of all trades gathered to await the arrival of the contractor and the beginning of the employment of men. A quartet of Negroes in the crowd began singing, causing the closing in of the crowd shown at the center of the picture. The only definitely employed men in sight appeared to be the street cleaner, at the forefront of the picture. The crowd, for the most part, was hopeful and jovial. Frank Messer, president of the construction company in charge, said work would begin next week.

Fig. 9. *Hundreds of Laborers Wait on Post Office Site.* From the *Nashville Banner,* June 6, 1933.

The appropriation for the new post office was $1.565 million. Nashville got such a large piece of the federal pie because its congressional representative, Joseph Byrns, was an influential member of the House Committee on Appropriations and was soon to become House Majority Leader.

LOCATION, LOCATION, LOCATION

The mantra beloved by real estate agents sums up the rationale for the Nashville Post Office site. "In 1930, the peak year for mail by rail, more than 10,000 trains were used to move the mail into every city, town, and village in the United States."[15] The Assistant Secretary of the Treasury who was in charge of the public building program, Ferry K. Heath, logically concluded that "[t]he most efficient mail service possible at Nashville requires that the new building shall be located in close proximity to the railroad station handling the bulk of the mail."[16] The loading platform problem at

the Customs House required larger quarters. But "so far as the immediate needs of the postal service are concerned, the present space is sufficient. . . . However, there is immediate and urgent need for more and a better loading platform [*sic*]. . . . To remedy the platform situation . . . it will therefore be necessary to purchase the property at the rear of the building and make the necessary extensions."[13]

An act of Congress in July 1930—before the collapse of Caldwell and Company—appropriated $205,000 for the acquisition of land adjacent to the Nashville Customs House, with an additional sum for construction of an extension not to exceed $500,000.

By February 1931 Congress had added $330 million to the original $175 million in the federal building till—obviously not because the federal government's space needs had multiplied that significantly, but because the construction industry had slumped so dramatically (fig. 9). In March 1931 the Treasury Department's assistant secretary began advertising for 82,500 square feet of land in Nashville "permitting direct contact with the mailing platform of the Union Station."[14]

Fig. 10. *Broadway, Showing the Site of the Future Post Office,* ca. 1919 (Veterans Arriving Home after World War I). From Joe Sherman, *A Thousand Voices: The Story of Nashville's Union Station* (Nashville, Tenn., ca. 1987). **Before clearance for the post office in 1933, the site was occupied by two small hotels, a fruit stand, and other small businesses that served the salesmen who rode the rails.**

the Customs House would not be an issue at the new post office. Mail could move from Union Station to the post office without the need for a fleet of trucks.

Because of the configuration of the site of Union Station, which is flanked on the west by the low-lying Gulch filled with train tracks, a post office located to the east was the only real possibility. That site was occupied by two small hotels patronized by salesmen who rode the rails—the Hotel Windsor and Regent's Hotel—as well as by Anthony de Matteo Fruits and auto and tire stores.[17] The ownership of this block was divided among a number of interests, including such well-known Nashville names as Edwin Warner, Luke Lea, and the Braid family, as well as one J. M. Coombs, who operated a pie wagon on the site (fig. 10).[18]

The inevitability of the post office site made negotiations for it difficult. Unusual for the Depression, it was a sellers' market. Some of the property owners demanded more than the appraised value, and the federal government was forced to condemn parcels to clear the buildings on them. Litigation dragged on until 1934, when the post office itself was nearing completion. Luke Lea, an intimate partner in the bankrupt Caldwell and Company, was in flight from the law, his assets under siege by creditors. To acquire the Coombs land, the government granted Coombs permission to operate his pie wagon on a corner of the construction site for the next eighteen months. The presence of the pie wagon made complete excavation of the site impossible and later caused the contractor to petition the government for damages caused by the delay.

It was not only owners of the designated site who proved difficult. The shift from the Customs House drew howls of protest from those who had stood to benefit from an addition to it. Members of the men's club Cumberland Lodge No. 8 F. & A. M., which owned the parcels immediately south of the Customs House where the extension had been planned, complained of the government's extravagance to everyone in Washington they could think of, including the Secretary of the Treasury, Ogden Mills.

The [post office] now being proposed in this city is a flagrant and unwarranted waste of public funds in view of the condition of the Treasury [$2 billion in debt]; it is not needed in the second place even if the Treasury was able to pay for it; and it has not been demanded by public sentiment in Nashville in the third place. The public is well aware of these facts and they are being discussed every day.

While your great office may not have control of the policy of locating and building post-offices, it is, as we understand, charged with seeing that the funds are wisely invested and properly spent.

If the government desires to reduce expenses, it can easily and properly save One Million Dollars here and not hurt anyone.[19]

And in the process help some.

But if the land acquisition lurched along, the design and construction of the post office moved fairly quickly. On November 5, 1931, the Nashville firm of Marr & Holman, Architects was selected to design the building, subject to the specifications of the Treasury Department's Office of the Supervising Architect. On February 4, 1932, members of the Marr & Holman office were in Washington, presenting plans and elevations for the building, which were approved by the supervising architect the following day. The federal government acquired title to the property in October 1932. In the spring of 1933, final construction drawings were approved, Frank Messer and Sons of Cincinnati were hired as the contractors, and by April 1933, site clearance was under way (fig. 11).

In June 1933 over a thousand workers lined up for construction jobs on the post office project (see fig. 9). The union scale wages they were seeking ranged from 22½ cents per hour for "laborers" to $1 per hour for the skilled trades—bricklayers and masons, steelworkers and tile setters.

The draftsmen who temporarily swelled the ranks of Marr & Holman during the post office project protested bitterly to the Secretary of Labor and the supervising architect that the pay they were receiving—$100 to $125 per

Fig. 11. *Site of the Future Nashville Post Office from the Southeast, June 30, 1933.* Photograph. Marr & Holman Collection, Tennessee Historical Society, Tennessee State Library & Archives.

Fig. 12. *The Nashville Post Office under Construction from the Northeast, January 2, 1934.* Photograph. Marr & Holman Collection, Tennessee Historical Society, Tennessee State Library & Archives.

month—was half of what they had been paid for similar work elsewhere. Many of these men were essentially itinerant architects, traveling from Michigan to Indiana to Georgia and Florida—wherever work was available, much of it post office design.

Changes in specified materials due to cost or to availability—from Tennessee to Georgia marble, from aluminum to steel for the spandrels between the windows—caused temporary hitches in the schedule. But the Office of the Supervising Architect pushed the architects and contractors relentlessly (fig. 12). The Nashville Post Office opened for business on November 26, 1934, eighteen months after the start of actual construction. It had taken six years to build Nashville's previous post office, the Customs House.[20]

THE FEDERAL STYLE

The construction of the Nashville Post Office proceeded relatively quickly, in part because the Office of the Supervising Architect allowed Marr & Holman no great leeway in the building's design. From before the Civil War through the 1930s, buildings constructed by the federal government around the country had an official style, courtesy of the Office of the Supervising Architect. The supervising architects were part of the Treasury Department's Office of Construction. The government's money handlers were responsible for the design, construction, and maintenance of most nonmilitary federal buildings, because the majority of federal functions housed in these mixed-use buildings generated revenue for the government.

The preferences of the federal architects were apparent in the federal buildings they designed. Robert Mills (1836–42) relied on Greek Revival forms, while Ammi B. Young (1842–62) favored the Renaissance Revival style. But some variety of classical inspiration remained in order, in part because of prevailing architectural fashion, in part because the majority of federal building was in Washington, D.C., where the classical tradition was especially strong.

After the Civil War, Congress authorized appropriations for a massive national building spree, and the Office of the

Supervising Architect grew to include administrators and engineers as well as architects. Their role, at a time when architects were only gradually beginning to define themselves as professionals, was to provide the government with well-made buildings at civil service salaries. The office eliminated the haphazard use of local architects, streamlining the planning and construction process into a veritable assembly line for blueprints.

Because of the centralized control of design and construction, a certain standardization set in. But conformity was the point. A courthouse is a courthouse, and a post office is a post office—they both had the same functional requirements regardless of geography. But the eclecticism of Victorian taste wrapped these similar functions in different historical skins when the supervising architect changed. For example, Alfred B. Mullett (1865–74) was fond of sprawling Second Empire piles, most notably the State, War, and Navy Building one block west of the White House. William Potter, the supervising architect who followed Mullett and designed Nashville's Customs House, did several similar Gothic town halls throughout the country during his three-year tenure.[21]

The classical tradition returned to official favor in 1901. In his annual report of that year, Supervising Architect James Knox Taylor gave the classical style his stamp of approval for federal buildings. The rationale: classicism was grounded in the support of institutional values through recognizable architectural symbols.

This was the age of the great conglomerates, the trusts of railroads, steel, electricity, oil, money, and securities that consolidated the means of production into massive mechanisms. It was also an age in which our culture was marked by imperial wars in Cuba and the Philippines, and by anxiety aroused by new waves of immigration.

The search for order in a culture becoming increasingly more complex needed an architecture to follow suit, and the symmetry and balance of classicism were ideally suited for this purpose. The full-blown classicism of the early Roman Empire took center stage as the best way to symbolize the

ONCE UPON A TIME THERE WAS AN OCEAN

The excavation of the site for the post office yielded more than 25,000 cubic feet of clay and rock for a fill in North Nashville. The excavators also blasted out a piece of Nashville's prehistoric past.

In September 1933 newspapers reported the discovery of the fossilized impression of a wormlike creature in a fragment of limestone removed from a depth of 20 feet to make way for the post office basement (fig. 13). State geologist W. F. Pond identified the foot-long specimen as a "cephalopod," a sea animal that lived in the shallow sea covering Middle Tennessee 400 million years ago. Pond explained that millions of cephalopoda—some as long as 15 feet—teemed in the warm waters that extended north from the Gulf of Mexico, creeping along the ocean floor by means of octopus-like tentacles near their mouths. The geologist also stated that the closest surviving relative to the ancient mollusk is the chambered nautilus of the Indian Ocean.

The impression of the post office cephalopod endured because the shell of the animal became embedded in the lime-ooze that covered the sea floor, and millions of years later crystallized into limestone. (information from the *Sunday Tennessean*, September 3, 1933)

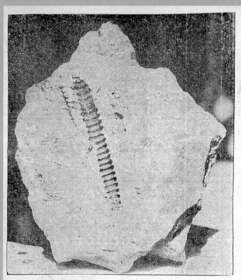

Here is the rock blasted from the postoffice site showing the impression of the ancient sea animal which once encrusted itself there.

Fig. 13. *Fossil of a Cephalopod Found during Foundation Blasting for the Future Nashville Post Office*. Limestone; dimensions of fossil ca. 12 × 1 in. From the *Sunday Tennessean*, September 3, 1933, magazine section, morning edition, 3.

grandeur, prosperity, and power of the now-mature American republic. The appetite for classical orders reflected a desire that the country march into the new century in a dignified and stately manner, perhaps because beneath the surface of self-confidence lay an unease about just where the country was rushing at such speed.

STRIPPED CLASSICISM

We venture to predict that the good architecture of the future will be done by Traditionalists practicing Moderne, or by Modernists practicing Traditionalle. Note this prediction. Bets to be collected on Labor Day, 1951.

—Edwin B. Morris, Federal Architect 1, no. 1
   (July 1930): 4

After the economic collapse of 1929, which called into question the viability of the economic system and the republican form of government of the United States, there was an even greater need for government architecture to support "institutional values." But 1930s federal classicism—the style of the Nashville Post Office—was not one of pediments and columns and capitals in the Greek orders. That kind of classicism was compromised by the government's need for speedy construction—to put the unemployed in the construction trades to work—and by the influence of the then-current International Style.

As early as the 1920s, an architectural import known generically as modernism had begun to eclipse the popularity of classicism. Unlike the Victorians, who sought to deny the impact industrialism was having on their culture by utilizing architectural forms revived from medieval, preindustrial periods, the modernists embraced the unadorned functionalism of the machine as expressive of their age. Ironically, the machine-age aesthetic sprang from many of the same motives that had in the past produced a classical revival: the desire for rationality and order.

The International Style: Architecture since 1922—the book that accompanied the exhibition at the Museum of Modern Art in New York in 1931—is an iron-fisted manifesto on the whys of modernism. In the preface, museum director Alfred H. Barr writes, "Some of us who have been appalled by this chaos [of historicism] turn with the utmost interest and expectancy to the International Style. . . . The Style requires discipline and restraint, the will to perfect as well as the will to invent. And this is contrary to the American cult of individualism."[22]

Modernism put all architectural ornament into the dustbin. For the modernist, the form of buildings should follow their function just the way the forms of machines did. If a structure was supported by a steel frame rather than masonry walls, then the walls should reflect their non–load bearing function—usually in the form of a glass curtain hung from the steel grid. At their best, such buildings had a transparency and lightness that symbolized a decidedly twentieth-century style of clarity—the clarity of the internal combustion engine. Modernist architect Le Corbusier called them "machines for living." Traditionalists called them "dumb boxes," mute to the language of symbol and history.

The federal architect's position within the debate between traditional and modern was articulated, appropriately enough, in the pages of the *Federal Architect*. This quarterly first appeared in July 1930 and was published by the Association of Federal Architects, the body of government-employed architects and engineers—primarily residing in the Treasury's Office of the Supervising Architect—charged with overseeing the massive building program authorized by Congress. The point of the journal was to explain—primarily to the architectural professional—the whats, wheres, hows, and whys of the new federal buildings.

Editor Edwin Morris summarized the traditional vs. modern controversy of styles in the language of an almost impartial jury.

The objection to the Traditionalists is that in their buildings they use too much architectural language to express their idea, and to the Modernists that they don't use enough. . . . The fault with the extreme Traditionalist is that he is preoccupied with his vocabulary rather than with his thought. The fault

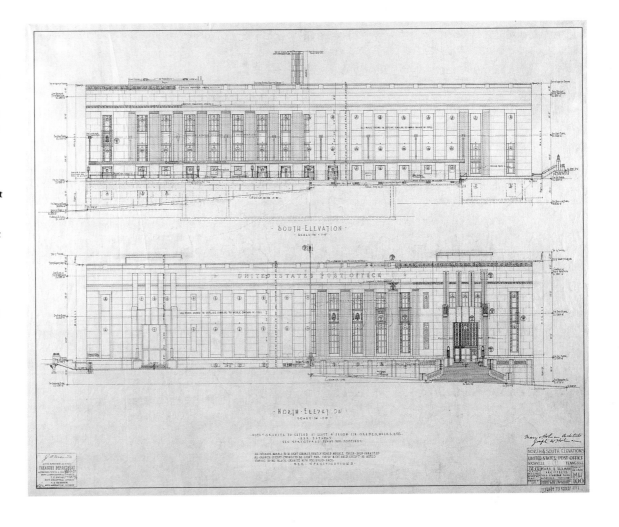

Fig. 14. Marr & Holman, Architects, *North and South Elevations of the Nashville Post Office.* Ink on linen; 31 × 39 in. Metropolitan Development and Housing Agency, on deposit with the Frist Center for the Visual Arts. **"Mr. Holman took immense pride in a job well done, and in the profession he was known as a stickler for details and demanded of his employees that drawings and specifications be thorough and complete. He was fully aware of the fact that most of the controversy between Architects and Contractors arose from the inadequacy of the drawings and specifications, and his insistence on thorough work generated good feelings in the construction industry."** (James Logan Howard, former Marr & Holman employee)

with the extreme Modernist (and there are too many of him) is that he has made a new dictionary with about nine words in it, and tries to talk intelligently and picturesquely by using only these nine.[23]

But there was never any real question that federal architecture would go wholeheartedly modern. For the federal government of the Depression, transparency and lightness were not appropriate symbols. Government needed to appear as a stable force in a decidedly unstable society. Federal architects were called on to express the values of permanence, rationality, and order—values that classicism served

so well—but in forms streamlined to suggest forward progress rather than looking backward. The synthesis of modern, traditional, and symbolic produced a classicism diluted in all these intents, scaled to serve a growing bureaucracy—the style known as "stripped" or even "starved" classicism.[24]

The Nashville Post Office is a textbook example of the stripped classical style (fig. 14). The basic form is a rectangle of horizontal rather than vertical dimensions—a stable mass, clear in outline, resting firmly on the earth. The steel frame of the building is veneered with massive slabs of a marble almost blindingly white, especially after its recent cleaning. These slabs are joined by surprisingly thin creases of mortar—much thinner than the mortar joints found in the typical brick building—that enhance the smooth, planar effect.

The windows are recessed between pilasters to diminish the interruption they make to the solidity of the block. The fluting of these pilasters and the rhythm they supply to the facade carry faint allusions to the Greek temple form. The peristyle, or single row of columns surrounding all four sides of Greek temples like the Parthenon, has in the case of the Post Office been drawn back into the facade, again so as not to detract from the planes of the walls.

The two entrance bays are placed symmetrically for balance and step outward from the facade to make access immediately apparent—a person does not have to be a government insider to figure out how the building works. Stalklike pilasters over the doors, as well as the pilasters of the central facade, provide a vertical thrust balancing the basic horizontality of the building. Note, however, that these verticals do not run the full height of the building. Racing off into the blue is for the skyscrapers of entrepreneurs, not for a rock-solid government.

Ornament is minimal. The ornate steel spandrels between the windows and grillwork over the doors are recessed into the walls rather than applied to them. The classical anthemion (honeysuckle) frieze is etched so delicately into the cornice as to suggest a light pencil drawing on paper.

This is an architecture of abstract simplification, in which the traditional ornament and articulation of classicism is absorbed by the massive wall, with its great planes and lines. The conspicuous consumption of the 1920s has been chastened, purified by a new discipline into a unifying order and vision (fig. 15; see fig. 2).

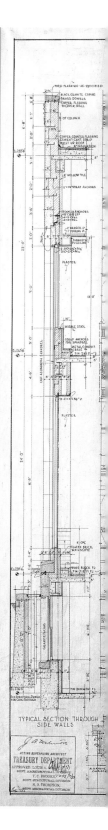

Fig. 15. Marr & Holman, Architects, *Exterior Wall Section and Main Details, Nashville Post Office.* Ink on linen; 31 × 39 in. Metropolitan Development and Housing Agency, on deposit with the Frist Center for the Visual Arts. **This Marr & Holman drawing has an Old World look that is not solely explained by age and the difference in materials and production—the human hand placing ink on linen vs. computer-generated images on paper. Architectural drawings from this period are often difficult for the contemporary eye to read. That is because they represent "typical" sections, do not spell out the repetition of every detail, and pack information into every inch of space.**

The architectural draftsman of the 1930s "filled the whole linen sheet—a piece of a section here, part of an elevation there, and details to take up the rest of the white space," says Seab Tuck, the architect of the renovation. "Today's architects don't do drawings like that at all.

"We don't put a floor plan and minute details on the same page," Tuck explains. "We'll pull them apart, onto separate sheets, so it's clearer just what the contractor or the subcontractor has to do. In the '30s you often find engineering documentation in architectural drawings, but today they're separate because the engineering is so much more complicated.

"When the post office was constructed," Tuck says, "you had craftsmen. That's not always the case today. A '30s drawing could show stone in a particular location, and the mason would automatically install it correctly. Today you're not sure how the stone will be installed. You have to make everything absolutely clear to make sure you get what's expected." (information from Seab A. Tuck III, interview by Christine Kreyling, July 7, 2000)

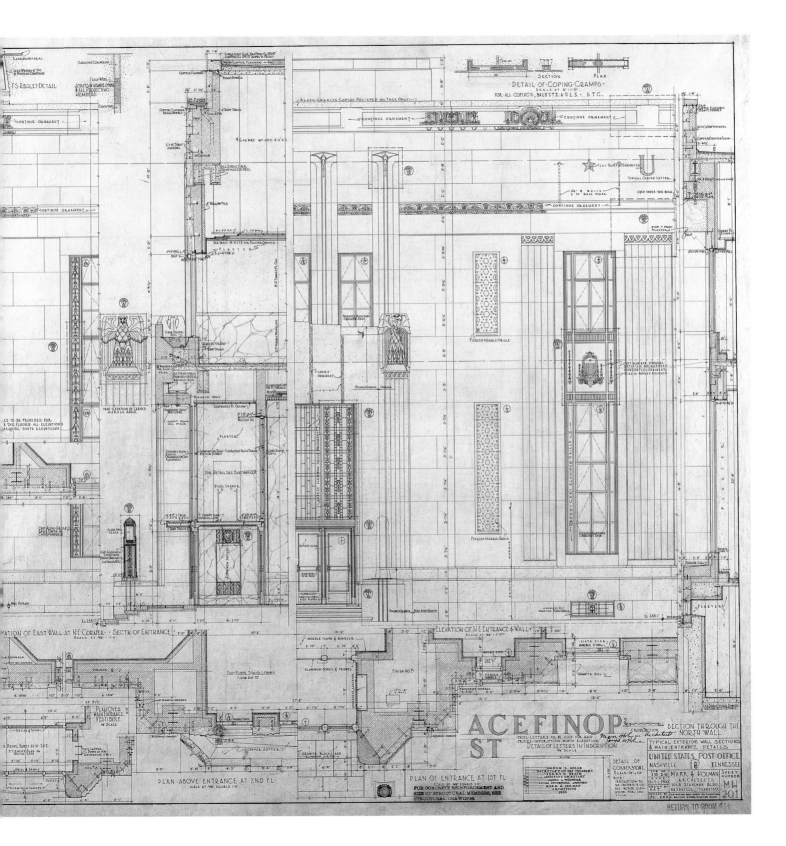

DETAIL OF COPING CRAMPS
SCALE AT 3"=1'-0"
FOR ALL COPINGS, BALUSTRADES, ETC.

ELEVATION OF EAST WALL AT N.E. CORNER & SECTN OF ENTRANCE
SCALE AT 3/8"=1'-0"

ELEVATION OF N.E. ENTRANCE & WALL
SCALE AT 3/8"=1'-0"

PLAN OVER MAIN ENTRANCE VESTIBULE
1/4" SCALE

PLAN ABOVE ENTRANCE AT 2ND FL.
SCALE AT 3/8" EQUALS 1'-0"

PLAN OF ENTRANCE AT 1ST FL.
SCALE AT 3/8" EQUALS 1'-0"
FOR CONCRETE REINFORCEMENT AND
SIZE OF STRUCTURAL MEMBERS, SEE
STRUCTURAL DRAWINGS.

ACEFINOP ST

THESE LETTERS TO BE USED FOR MAIN
FRIEZE INSCRIPTION NORTH ELEVATION
DETAIL OF LETTERS IN INSCRIPTION
3/4" SCALE

CROSS SECTION
SECTION THROUGH THE
NORTH WALL

TYPICAL EXTERIOR WALL SECTIONS
& MAIN ENTRANCE DETAILS

UNITED STATES POST OFFICE
NASHVILLE ⑧ TENNESSEE

MARR & HOLMAN
ARCHITECTS
1015 STAHLMAN BLDG.
NASHVILLE, TENNESSEE

SHEET
NUMBER
MH
201

OGDEN L. MILLS
SECRETARY OF THE TREASURY
FERRY K. HEATH
ASSISTANT SECRETARY
ACTING SUPERVISING ARCHITECT
MARR & HOLMAN
ARCHITECTS
1933

DETAIL OF
COMMISSION
SCALE 1/2"=1'-0"

Fig. 16. Baumann and Baumann, Architects, *The Knoxville Post Office and Courthouse*, 1934.

A comparison of Marr & Holman's Nashville Post Office with the Knoxville Post Office and Courthouse by the Knoxville firm of Baumann and Baumann points out the standardized designs for federal buildings that resulted from the control exercised by the Office of the Supervising Architect and the need for speedy construction to pump life into the depressed building trades (fig. 16). Both post offices were completed in 1934, occupy an entire city block, and have similar dimensions. The length of each is 250 feet. The Nashville Post Office is 182 feet deep, slightly greater than Knoxville's 138-foot depth. The Nashville structure contains 147,000 square feet of gross floor area, while Knoxville's has 123,000 square feet. The budgets for both buildings were slightly over $1.5 million.

But it is by looking, not by crunching numbers, that the striking similarities between the two buildings emerge most clearly. Kindred architectural envelopes convey powerful impressions of a stable but streamlined government capable of sustaining its citizens through the lean times of the Depression. The mass of both post offices is a rectangular block of strongly horizontal proportions, and the rhythms of the two front facades are almost identical. Knoxville's post office is scored with engaged fluted columns, while that of Nashville has flat fluted pilasters. These elements, rising the height of the windows recessed between them, divide the central portion into nine bays. Above the window openings runs a frieze of floriated design.

The entrance bays call attention to themselves in similar ways. Both extend out from the main block of the building and contain door surrounds of contrasting stone—gray-pink Minnesota granite in Nashville, red marble in Knoxville. The vertical elements flanking the entrances are topped by eagles, but of different design.

Architects were instructed by the Treasury Department to employ local, or at least regional, materials as much as possible, to pump much-needed dollars into local economies. For this reason, a pinkish East Tennessee marble was originally specified for both buildings. At the last minute, due to problems of supply, the facing of the Nashville Post Office was changed to a white Georgia marble. The stone that forms the base of each building is the same granite (Nashville) or marble (Knoxville) of the respective door surrounds; each establishes the same dark contrast with the light marble walls.

The almost identical dimensions and the Art Deco styling of both lobbies, which lie near the front of each main floor, further blur the distinctions. The materials of both are luxurious marbles, bronze, and cast aluminum. The stylized floral motifs of the aluminum grillwork are in some cases exactly the same pattern.

The main difference between the Nashville and Knoxville buildings is functional. In the 1930 census, Nashville had a population of 153,866, while Knoxville's was 105,802. More people means more postal business. That's why the Nashville building was dedicated solely to the mails, while Knoxville's was a mixed-use structure whose upper floors housed the federal courts. Today the Knoxville building continues to serve as both post office and courthouse.

"AIN'T THIS SWELL!"

—Remark by a young boy at the open house of the Nashville Post Office

The customers of the Nashville Post Office got their first chance to see their early Christmas present from Uncle Sam on Sunday, November 18, 1934. From 1 to 7 P.M., Postmaster William Gupton threw open the doors, even before the postal employees or equipment had moved from the Customs House down the street. An estimated 40,000 to 50,000 Nashvillians—families with children, dowagers in furs, elderly gents in their Sunday best—wandered through the lobby (fig. 17), up and down the marble stairs, into the walnut-paneled offices of the postmaster and his crew of supervisors, murmuring "wonderful," "magnificent," and "swell."

It was a red-letter day for Nashville. The Sunday *Tennessean* devoted many column inches to the story, describing not only the building and its history but the entire 138-year history of postal service in the city. The paper applauded the role of the New Deal in civic affairs, a role underlined by a flying visit to Nashville just the day before by President Franklin Roosevelt and the First Lady, on their way to inspect TVA sites in the region.

On hand to greet the gawkers was a phalanx of civic and business officials: Congressman Joseph Byrns—who was responsible for guiding the appropriation for the building through the House of Representatives—Mayor Hillary Howse, Judge Litton Hickman, representatives of the Chamber of Commerce and the railroads, and architect Joseph Holman. Contractor Frank Messer sounded almost as awe-struck as the crowd over the interior finishings. "There are between 3,500 and 4,000 [train]-car loads of marble in this building," he said, adding, "We tried to carry out what the architects wanted and the fact that Mr. Holman and I are still friends should speak for the results."[25]

Gupton explained to a *Tennessean* reporter that he had decided on an open house rather than a formal dedication

Fig. 18. *Allegorical Female Figure.* Northwest vestibule, Frist Center for the Visual Arts. Cast aluminum. **An Art Deco allegorical figure, holding the torch of liberty and the book of law: American liberty guaranteed by the rule of law.**

space on the north side of the vast distribution center of the Nashville Post Office, the place where citizens could meet and greet while conducting their postal commerce. Its deluxe treatment in a suave style with allusions to hotel lobbies and corporate offices—much more modish and less historicist than the severe classicism of the exterior facade—was a visual reminder that the business of government was a going concern during the years when the American economy was staggering.

The style of the lobby is what we now call Art Deco. The term comes from the title of an influential exhibition of decorative and industrial arts held in Paris in 1925: "L'Exposition Internationale des Arts Décoratifs et Industriels Modernes." World War I had damaged the French economy, which resulted in the decline of France as the arbiter of taste. The goal of the exposition was to put the nation back on top. Accordingly, the fair was organized exclusively around the decorative arts, and the rules governing the exhibits excluded designs closely based on historical styles.[28] (Until the 1960s, contemporary design of the 1920s and 1930s was referred to as Art Moderne in Europe, and Moderne or Modernistic in the United States. By whatever term, it was the latest thing.)

The Art Deco designer rejected historicism as inappropriate to the twentieth-century structure. In place of the Ionic volutes (scrolls) and acanthus leaves of classicism (e.g., the Tennessee State Capitol) and the Gothic quatrefoil and crocket (e.g., the Nashville Customs House), up-to-the-minute geometric and floral abstractions derived from Paris were introduced: chevrons, arcs, sunbursts, and nubile maidens (fig. 18). Art Deco buildings broke no new ground in planning or structure. Unlike the steel frame and glass curtain of the International Style, Art Deco modernity was strictly a matter of surface treatment.

But surface was as important as substance during the Depression. Sumptuous materials in forms streamlined to suggest an aggressive rushing toward progress were the federal government's answer to the question, "Buddy, can you spare a dime?"

because the laying of the cornerstone the year before had already made the building official. "Now everybody is taking a hand in it," Gupton said, "and they have a chance to feel that it really belongs to them."[26]

By all newspaper accounts, the luxurious lobby, especially its marble wastebaskets, was far and away the biggest hit. "No wonder it cost a million dollars. Yes, I said a million, Sarah," insisted one mother to her daughter, patting the walls of marbles from East Tennessee with exotic names like Phantasia Rose and Monte Neva.[27]

That the lobby excited the most admiration was appropriate; that's what it was designed to do. This was the public

ICONS OF AN ERA

The program of visual imagery embedded in the walls of the Nashville Post Office confirms the self-confidence of the building's architecture: federal government is a powerful centralized authority in an expanding economic empire. During the dark days of the Depression, the federal builders spared no rhetoric to reinforce Americans' confidence in their public institutions—and in themselves.

THE EAGLE: ICON OF A NATION

The search for symbols of national identity began even before the nation was fully established. On the same day as the signing of the Declaration of Independence, the Continental Congress voted to empower a triumvirate—John Adams, Benjamin Franklin, and Thomas Jefferson—to devise a seal for the just-proclaimed United States of America. Three more committees, two consulting artists, and six years later (in 1782), the design of the Great Seal was finally approved. The choice for the seal's central image was the American bald eagle (fig. 19).

In preferring the eagle to a figure representing Columbia—the classicized version of the Indian princess whom Europeans had long identified with the New World—the Founding Fathers combined the symbol for ancient Roman state power with the native fauna of America. On the seal the eagle bears a shield of stars and stripes, grasping in its talons the olive branch of peaceful intentions and the arrows of a strong national defense. From its beak floats the motto *E Pluribus Unum*: from many, one. For an upstart nation struggling for unity, such symbolism served as a visual rallying cry to a people whose social identities had been tied to diverse national origins—and whose loyalties were primarily local and regional.[29]

Fig. 19. *Great Seal of the United States.* Lobby, Frist Center for the Visual Arts. Aluminum.

35

The postal system itself has had three icons in its long history: first Mercury—the messenger of the gods in Roman mythology— then a post rider on horseback, and finally the national symbol of the eagle. The big bird was looking all too earthbound when the Postal Service Board of Governors hired Nashvillian Marvin Runyon as Postmaster General in 1992. "I was selected because when I ran the Tennessee Valley Authority, I'd turned it into a profit-making business," Runyon recalls. The postal service was hemorrhaging money and Runyon was supposed to stop it.

Runyon began by stressing to each and every one of the 850,000 postal employees that the post office "had customers— 125 million households receive mail delivery six days a week, 52 weeks a year—but we also had competitors. I wanted to put the 'service' back into the postal service." Then the new postmaster began looking for a new logo. The one he'd inherited featured what he describes as a "roosting eagle," which to Runyon just confirmed the perception of the U.S. mails as a bureaucracy too bloated to move with the times. He asked his designers for a bird in flight.

"We came up with several designs and conducted focus groups of postmasters from different cities to vote on their favorite," Runyon says. He got a consensus on one, but the postmasters were not instantly comfortable with the new symbolism. "The problem," they said, "is that we'll have to move faster, because the image connotes speed." That was exactly the postmaster's point. Today what Runyon calls the "sonic eagle" is the instantly recognizable icon for a postal system that is holding its own in the marketplace (fig. 20). (Marvin Runyon, interview by Christine Kreyling, July 6, 2000)

Fig. 20. *Logo of the U.S. Postal Service.* U.S. Postal Service, Broadway Station, Nashville, Tenn., 1999.

In the latter half of the nineteenth century, federal architects frequently employed eagles as symbolic shorthand to give their buildings a "federal" identity, which set them apart from similarly styled commercial buildings such as banks.[30] The four birds that stand like centurions at the entrances to the Nashville Post Office required no arrows or olive branches to remind a people brought to their economic knees that the nation—grounded with stable roots in the past—was still strong, still one (see fig. 2).

PROGRESS AND PRODUCTIVITY

The lobby was the consumer-affairs section of the Nashville Post Office. Its twelve aluminum icons reflect the civic commerce below, generic images that define the postal service in particular, and the American economy in general, as dynamic agents of progress and productivity. The mass-produced icons symbolize, through the means of their manufacture as well as their primarily technological subjects, the faith—especially intense in the United States—in the inevitable onward and upward spiral of mankind courtesy of the machine. "If the machine was the icon of this era," writes historian James Draeger, "buildings [such as the Post Office] were its temples."[31] "'The reality of our century is technology,' proclaimed the artist Moholy-Nagy, 'the invention, construction, and maintenance of the machine. To be a user of the machine is to be of the spirit of this century. It has replaced the transcendental spiritualism of past eras.'"[32]

After the stock market crash, architectural decoration was pared down as the drive to reduce production costs accelerated. Handcraft, already on the decline because of the advances made in mass production during World War I, had become too expensive. Simplicity and standardization were the keys. Designers concentrated on streamlined forms that could be machine made at reasonable prices and still satisfy a high aesthetic standard. And the age of metal began to phase out the age of terracotta and stone in architectural ornament. The material's inherent sleekness seemed more in harmony with a swiftly moving world.[33]

PLANES, TRAINS, AND AUTOMOBILES

The frieze of four icons illustrating an airplane, a locomotive, a ship, and an automobile represents the speed and power of transportation harnessed to deliver the mail (figs. 21–24). This grouping logically appears within the motion corridors—the areas people move through, near the entrance–exits—of the building.

But these icons symbolize a proud postal history as well as then-current technology, according to the official *History of the United States Postal Service*.

The Postal Service has helped develop and subsidize every new mode of transportation in the United States. The postal role was a natural one: apart from postal employees themselves, transportation was the single most important element in mail delivery, literally, the legs of communication. Even when the general public was skeptical or fearful of a new means of transportation, postal officials experimented with inventions that offered potential for moving the mail faster.

As mail delivery evolved from foot to horseback, stagecoach, steamboat, railroad, automobile, and airplane, with intermediate and overlapping use of balloons, helicopters, and pneumatic tubes, mail contracts ensured the income necessary to build the great highways, rail lines, and airways that eventually spanned the continent.

In 1831, when steam-driven engines . . . were denounced as a "device of Satan to lead immortal souls to hell," railroads began to carry mail. . . . As early as 1896 the Post Office Department experimented with the "horseless wagon," in its search for faster and cheaper carriage. . . . The Post Office Department authorized its first experimental air flight in 1911.

One transportation technology, however, remains only a footnote in the history of mail delivery. On June 8, 1959, in a move a postal official heralded as "of historic significance to the peoples of the entire world," the Navy submarine U.S.S. Barbero fired a guided missile carrying 3,000 letters to the Naval Auxiliary Air Station in Mayport, Florida. "Before man reaches the moon," the official was quoted as saying, "mail will be delivered within hours from New York to California, to Britain, to India or Australia by guided missiles."[34]

"The Postal Service made this country," echoes former Postmaster General Marvin Runyon. "For 225 years it forged

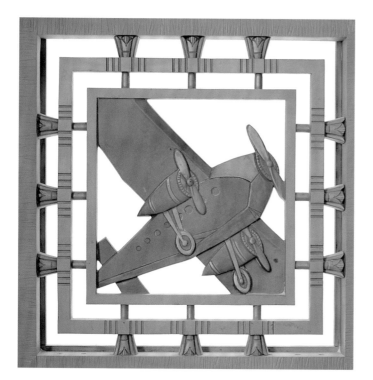 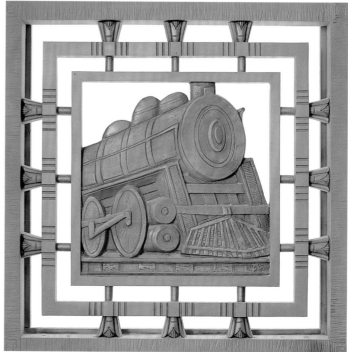

Fig. 21. *Airplane.* Cast aluminum. Lobby, Frist Center for the Visual Arts.

Fig. 22. *Locomotive.* Cast aluminum. Lobby, Frist Center for the Visual Arts.

Fig. 23. *Ship.* Cast aluminum. Lobby, Frist Center for the Visual Arts.

Fig. 24. *Automobile.* Cast aluminum. Lobby, Frist Center for the Visual Arts. **Transportation is the legs of postal communication. And the postal service has subsidized the expansion of every new mode in the United States. As mail delivery evolved from foot and horseback to ships and railroads, automobiles and airplanes, mail contracts fed the investment in the great highways, rail lines, and airways that ultimately spanned the continent.**

communication channels, which is what allowed the United States to progress so rapidly." Runyon points out that today the post office is the largest user of environmentally sensitive electric- and propane-powered vehicles in the country. And during his tenure (1992–98), the postal service began to study hovercraft to deliver mail in the extremely icy conditions of Alaska, where dogsleds had been used to deliver mail until 1963. "In Alaska, because there are so few roads," Runyon explains, "they build houses by mail, ship bricks by mail."

Runyon wryly notes that people began sounding the death knell of the post office first with the invention of the railroad, and then with the telephone, and then with the telex. "About fifteen or so years ago," Runyon recalls, "Congress did a study on the life expectancy of the post office. Since then it's tripled in size. Nothing can replace the mails. You can't open up a box of cookies from your grandmother, or a perfumed envelope, with e-mail."[35]

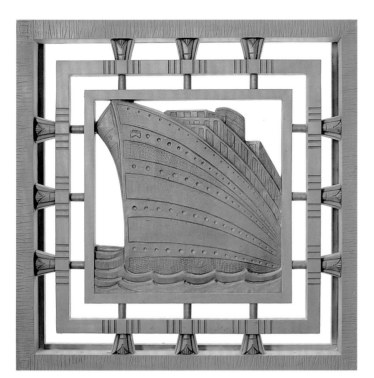

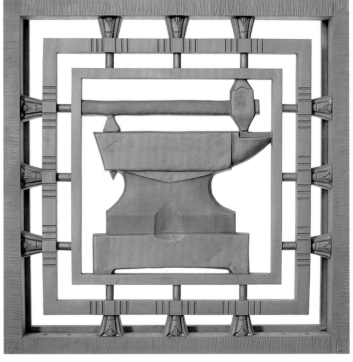

Fig. 25. *Plow.* Cast aluminum. Lobby, Frist Center for the Visual Arts. **The plow that turned a wilderness into fields that fed the country.**

Fig. 26. *Anvil.* Cast aluminum. Lobby, Frist Center for the Visual Arts. **The anvil forged the iron that shod the plowhorse that built the rails.**

Fig. 27. *Books and Lamp.* Cast aluminum. Lobby, Frist Center for the Visual Arts. **The books of wisdom topped by the lamp of learning.**

Fig. 28. *Dolphin and Propeller.* Cast aluminum. Lobby, Frist Center for the Visual Arts. **The dolphin is an ancient symbol of swift passage through the seas, and the propeller the man-made equivalent.**

MEANS OF PRODUCTION

The two friezes of four icons repeated in the grillwork of the main lobby represent the tools used throughout the nation's history to craft its economic and cultural prosperity (figs. 25–32). The motifs are essentially two-dimensional; their precision, regular recurrence, and metallic cast, as much as their subjects, symbolize machine production.

The groupings delineate no connected narrative but rather present agriculture and industry, science and learning, in democratically comprehensible images. Taken collectively they form an allegory of forward motion, industrial progress, and hope for economic revival.

 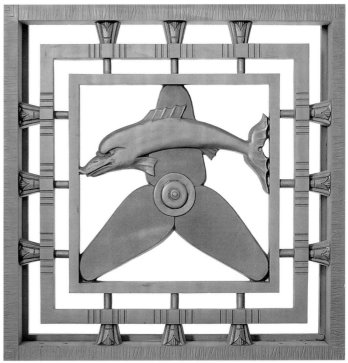

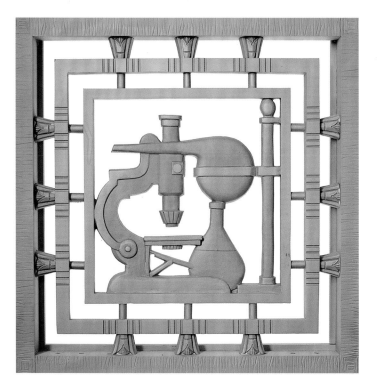 

Fig. 29. *Microscope and Beaker.* Cast aluminum. Lobby, Frist Center for the Visual Arts. **Tools of scientific exploration.**

Fig. 30. *Sickle and Wheat.* Cast aluminum. Lobby, Frist Center for the Visual Arts. **Ancient symbols of the harvest.**

Fig. 31. *Gears.* Cast aluminum. Lobby, Frist Center for the Visual Arts. **Symbols of the precision of industrial progress.**

Fig. 32. *Printing Press.* Cast aluminum. Lobby, Frist Center for the Visual Arts. **The mechanical means that democratized knowledge.**

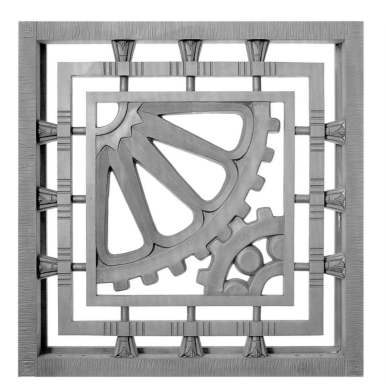

PAGEANT OF PROGRESS

The icons of the 1934 post office were not the first instance in Nashville of the identification of transportation modes with the delivery of the U.S. mail. On July 24, 1925, Nashville Postmaster William O'Callaghan staged a "Pageant of Progress" to celebrate the 150th anniversary of the U.S. Postal Department. O'Callaghan invited various business organizations to create floats showing the steps of progress that had been taken in the postal service from the appointment of Benjamin Franklin as the first Postmaster General by the Continental Congress in 1775 to the present.

Nashvillians thronged to the 2-mile-long parade, clogging the sidewalks along Broadway, cheering the letter carriers' band. A horseback rider, stagecoach, Alaskan dog team, motorcycle, automobile, and three airplanes flying over the line of march represented the various historic and current vehicles used to transport the mails. One float designed by postal employees featured a coffin containing an exhibit to represent the expiration of the dead letter, accompanied by an actual hearse to symbolize the burial of the phenomenon. Another exhibit showed the correct way to address a letter.

Marching in the parade were two congressmen, the mayor of Nashville, and a host of postal officials past and present—including 99-year-old Edward Lee, the postmaster for Columbia, Tennessee, from 1854 to 1857. That evening a large banquet was sponsored by the Chamber of Commerce to demonstrate the close ties between the postal service and the business of America. (information from Harry S. New, *United States Official Postal Guide*, 4th ser., 5, no. 3 [Washington, D.C.: Post Office Department, September 1925], 1, 2)

WHERE ARE THE MURALS?

Art lovers familiar with the New Deal period walk into the lobby of the 1934 Nashville Post Office and wonder why there are no murals. They recall the democratic vistas that adorn the walls of post offices and other government buildings of the 1930s—scenes of cranberry pickers in Massachusetts and harvesters in Missouri and loggers in Michigan, by artists such as Guy Pène du Bois and Philip Guston and Ben Shahn. If the post office was intended as an affirmation of the work ethic during a time when the reality was unemployment, why does the building not have the pictures to prove it?

The answer is one of timing. The Nashville Post Office was essentially a product of the Hoover administration. The building was already designed and under construction during the winter of 1933–34, when the federal government made its first foray into art patronage, employing painters, sculptors, and printmakers to make art for the masses. It was the later Roosevelt administration that established more ambitious programs to aid artists on relief and decorate government buildings.

The Federal Arts Project of the Works Progress (later Work Projects) Administration (1935–43) commissioned unemployed artists—primarily in large cities, where most of them lived—to make works destined for state and municipal institutions. To provide decorations for federal buildings, the Treasury Department, which built and administered these structures, established a Section of Painting and Sculpture, later called the Section of Fine Arts (1934–43). Through the Section of Fine Arts, artists were commissioned to craft the images of peacefulness and productivity that grace the walls of so many Depression-era post offices. By virtue of its earlier timing, however, the Nashville Post Office was designed without murals. (information from Marlene Park and Gerald E. Markowitz, *Democratic Vistas: Post Offices and Public Art in the New Deal* [Philadelphia: Temple University Press, 1984], 6)

MARR & HOLMAN, ARCHITECTS

God closed my ears to the petty noises of the world that I might better envision beautiful buildings.

—Thomas Marr, quoted in Mrs. J. B. Chandler, "Thomas Scott Marr, Architect," *Silent Worker*, June 1929, 185

In retrospect it seems a case of kismet that the firm of Marr & Holman designed the Nashville Post Office. For it was the preceding Nashville post office that inspired Thomas Marr (1866–1936) to become an architect. As a child the partially deaf Marr sat on the front steps of his home for hours and hours, watching the stonemasons lay the blocks for the Nashville Custom House, Courthouse, and Post Office across the street. He was fascinated by the visual spectacle before him, Marr later recalled to James Howard, an engineer with the Marr & Holman office from 1928 to 1943. "As the Federal Building progressed, Mr. Marr became interested to the extent that he decided upon a career as an Architect," Howard writes, "pursuing this interest through Gallaudet College [a school for the hard of hearing in Washington, D.C.] for his technical training . . . and upon graduation returning to Nashville to establish his practice."[36]

Marr worked for various architectural firms—taking time off to study architecture for a year at the Massachusetts Institute of Technology, in Cambridge—before opening his own firm around the turn of the century. His deafness and a consequent speech impediment made conversing with clients difficult. So Marr set up as a one-man shop—no other draftsmen or even a secretary—and focused almost exclusively on residential design, sometimes earning as little as $25 for a cottage plan.[37]

When Marr hired Joseph Holman (1890–1952) in 1905, he was to be a part-time office boy, running errands and sweeping up for $3.50 per week. But Holman brought with him not only an interest in architecture and engineering but the ears to hear of projects up for grabs and the tongue to charm clients into contracts. In 1913 (some sources say 1910[38]) the two formed a partnership, with Holman responsible for marketing, client relations, and negotiating contracts, while Marr did most of the design work.

Holman was an aggressive marketeer, using family connections—such as his brother-in-law, a prominent Nashville surgeon—and influential friends to secure new business. "It is not generally known by laymen, and the public in general [but Holman knew full well], that Architects are selected on the basis of merit, experience, and pressure put on those vested with the responsibility of making a selection," Howard writes.[39]

Holman talked the firm into becoming one of the most productive in Nashville (fig. 33). During the Roaring Twenties, the office in the Stahlman Building churned out a steady stream of blueprints: theaters for the Crescent Amusement Company; stores and warehouses for H. G. Hill & Company; dormitories for the University of the South; garages and automobile showrooms, hotels and offices, and lots of government projects—the Tennessee Home and Training School for the Feeble-Minded, the Tennessee School for the Deaf, the Federal Reserve Bank of Atlanta. "Mr. Holman realized that he must become politically involved in the interest of securing work from the Federal, State, City, and County governments," Howard writes, "and he was successful to the extent that much of the firm's work came from these sources."[40]

One of four offices of Mar and Holman in Stahlman Building, Nashville, Tenn. Mr. Marr, on the right is discussing a building plan with his partner.

Fig. 33. *The Architects at Work.* From Mrs. J. B. Chandler, "Thomas Scott Marr, Architect," *Silent Worker,* June 1929, 183.

Even before the Depression reduced all but government construction from a flow to a trickle, Holman lobbied elected officials hard, not only for his firm but also for his family. As early as 1913 Holman was writing to Nashville's Joseph Byrns, a member of the influential Committee on Appropriations in the House of Representatives, asking for the congressman's help in securing the Nashville position of inspector of railway post equipment—or at least "something in the local post office"—for his father.[41] Dogged in his efforts, he sent a follow-up letter to Byrns, asking "of just what does the examination [for the position] consist?" and explaining, "I am very anxious to get something for father that will put him on the inside" instead of working outdoors. "I hope I can repay you for these favors."[42]

Whether Holman ever repaid Byrns is an open question, but there is plenty of evidence in Marr & Holman correspondence that Holman went back to the governmental well again and again. A 1915 appeal to Byrns for help in securing the contract for the state's Cookeville Polytechnic School reveals the pragmatic nature of his pitch. "As you know, the selection of an architect is largely a matter of personality, just merely the *capable* fellow with the proper amount of

influence [emphasis Holman's]."[43] Byrns's response to "Dear Joe" later that month was equally to the point: "Glad to help."[44]

In hunting out work for the firm, Holman indulged what Howard describes as his "extravagant personal habits of travel and entertainment," preferring to travel by plane even in the early days of aviation and sending out for scotch—Haig & Haig—to lubricate the deals on the table in his hotel room.[45] And he was shrewd in tailoring his presentation to fit the fashions of his audience. When Mr. Holman went to Washington, which was frequently, "he carried in his baggage spats, a walking cane, and a homburg hat"—apparel he never wore in the more conservative sartorial climate of Nashville—and set up headquarters at the fancy Mayflower Hotel.[46]

Holman's aggressive business acumen and outgoing manner perfectly complemented his senior partner's more retiring character. Bachelor Marr was content to remain at the drafting table, live quietly, and travel little, preferring a family retreat at Beersheba Springs—from which he would send huckleberries for office consumption[47]—to the bright lights of the big city.

Architectural practice during the 1920s and 1930s, when Marr & Holman was in its heyday, made no great division between the professions of architecture and engineering, and placed limited emphasis on uniqueness of design—at least outside the major urban centers. Architecture was a business, not a fine art, and the nature of Marr & Holman reflects this ethos.

"The firm always operated as Architects and Engineers, performing the mechanical, electrical, structural, civil, and sanitary engineering . . . 'in house' with no outside consultants."[48] Much of the firm's success, according to Howard, resulted from staff engineer Richard Reynolds's "ability to master all phases of engineering work as related to the firm's practice."[49] When the volume of work periodically increased, Holman used his wide acquaintance with architects in other cities to borrow draftsmen from their firms until the tide ebbed.

Marr & Holman did not nurture a stable of designers bent on establishing a signature style. Design was largely a question of surveying the latest building types and styles throughout the country and incorporating current developments into the firm's projects. "Mr. Holman had an enormous retentive memory, and in visiting various buildings in other cities he could reconstruct from memory the exterior and interior details and the materials used, all of which was quite useful in executing the design of projects undertaken," Howard explains.[50] Marr & Holman preferred a popular definition of functionality to the "form follows function" aesthetic of the avant-garde International Style. According to Howard, "Mr. Holman once remarked, concerning buildings designed by the firm, that if the roof did not leak, and the heating system worked, then the building was a success."[51]

Perhaps it was this practicality and business savvy that made Marr & Holman the exception when most of the architectural firms in Nashville closed their doors, or took projects outside the profession, during the early 1930s (fig. 34). National statistics were equally grim. Nearly one-half of all architectural firms failed in 1930; by 1932 the survivors had

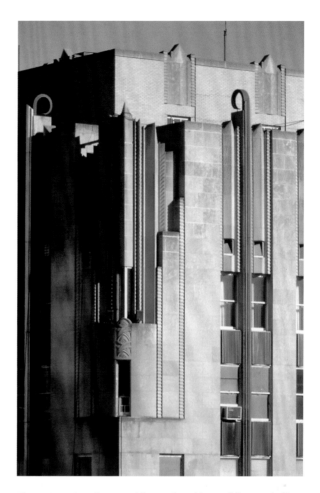

Fig. 34. Marr & Holman, Architects, *The Sudekum Building*, Nashville, 1932. **Joseph Holman's friendship with Tony Sudekum led to a great deal of work for Marr & Holman, including the Sudekum Building. As stockholders in Tony Sudekum's Crescent Amusement Company, Marr & Holman designed theaters for the chain throughout the Southeast.**

The structure was originally called the Warner Building, because Warner Brothers bought out Sudekum's interest during the planning stage. Joseph Holman went to Warner's New York office to retain the commission, and Marr & Holman became the first Southern architects ever employed by a national theater chain. The original plan included a theater, which was not completed until 1952 due to the Depression and World War II.

The principal designer of the Sudekum Building was Henry Horneman, a recent German immigrant borrowed from a Chicago firm by Joseph Holman. The 12-story steel-and-concrete structure, with its streamlined aluminum strips curved over the parapet to catch the sun's rays, was demolished in 1992.

Fig. 35. Marr & Holman, Architects. *The Belle Meade Theater*, Nashville, 1936. The rising popularity of the automobile in the 1920s and 1930s reversed the trend of increased density in the urban core in favor of suburban development. Theater entrepreneur Tony Sudekum approached Marr & Holman with plans for a movie theater and shopping strip on Harding Road, near the upscale Belle Meade subdivision. The concept was a large movie house with a prominent marquee and pylon for visibility to drive-by traffic and a series of attached setback shops. The materials: porcelain, aluminum, and glass for sleekness, and lots of neon to make the building a billboard.

The Belle Meade theater gained Marr & Holman national attention. *Architectural Record*'s 50th-anniversary issue presented the Streamlined Moderne complex as one of the nation's best new shopping centers. The building is now occupied by the Bookstar chain.

less than one-seventh of the work architects had enjoyed in the last boom year, 1928.[52]

The collapse of the Caldwell and Company bond empire in November 1930, which brought the Depression to Nashville, undoubtedly hurt the firm. Marr & Holman had served as consulting architects to the company's real estate mortgage bond division since 1923, receiving many commissions as a result of this connection, and secured financing through Caldwell for projects such as the Andrew Jackson Hotel. Holman had also offered access to Caldwell financing to other firms in the South, in exchange for making Marr & Holman a partner in the projects.[53]

That Marr & Holman was able to continue, albeit with a reduced staff, when all around them were going under, was due in large part to the Nashville Post Office—specifically its $1.5 million budget, of which the firm took the fee typical for the time of 3 percent. The $800,000 construction cost alone was greater than the sum of all other building permits in the city for the entire year of 1933.[54]

Such a prize was the object of intense competition among Nashville architects. In March 1931, even before the call for architects was officially announced, letters and portfolios began pouring into the Treasury Department. Every local firm left standing amid the rubble of the ruined construction industry pulled out all the stops, pressuring bankers and attorneys, university administrators and business executives with influence in Washington to write in their support. The local chapter of the American Legion demanded that the Treasury Department contract with one of its members for the job. Nashville Postmaster O. F. Minton sent letters in support of two different firms.

Politicians were especially hard hit. Nashville mayor Hillary Howse wrote on behalf of Henry Hibbs, the designer of Scarritt College and other academic buildings at Vanderbilt University. Kenneth McKellar, the U.S. Senate powerhouse from Memphis, also petitioned for Hibbs. Senator Cordell Hull sent letters for Hibbs, as well as for classicist Donald Southgate. Congressman Byrns, Holman's old friend, sent not only two letters in favor of Marr & Holman but separate missives for three other firms as well.

Holman made one of his jaunts to the national capital to call personally on the Treasury's acting supervising architect, James Wetmore.[55] If he used his father as part of his efforts to secure the contract, it was not the first time. "In one instance," Howard recalls, "one member of a Building committee was a Postman, and [Holman] emphasized to this individual that he [Holman] was the son of a Postman, result being that he wound up with the job."[56]

Eight months after the barrage started, all fell quiet on the Nashville front. On November 5, 1931, Treasury Secretary William Woodin named Marr & Holman as architects for the Nashville Post Office.

By the time that Holman was lobbying Wetmore, and anyone else in Washington who would listen, for the post office commission, Marr was semiretired. Howard recalls that "he spent the days in a rocking chair in the corner of Mr. Holman's office, doing very little work in the drafting room."[57] The Marr & Holman architect placed in charge of the post office design was Harry Dinkins, whom Howard describes as "a self-made Architect, a floater so to speak, having worked in New Mexico, Texas, and Louisiana."[58]

Marr & Holman could use a self-made designer on such a big project because Dinkins did not have to start from scratch. The Treasury Department outlined rigid specifications for the design of post offices, in part because of the technological complexity of postal service, in part because of the desire for speed of construction. The department had a massive congressional appropriation to spend and the federal government wanted to put as many construction workers on the payroll as quickly as possible. The solution —to standardize the architectural product in the manner of an assembly line—left little flexibility for architectural discretion. Marr & Holman, which routinely worked from commercial prototypes, shifted easily to a governmental one.

After the construction of the Nashville Post Office, alongside some local projects (fig. 35), more government work kept Marr & Holman afloat through the Depression. The New Deal's Public Works Administration doled out dollars to state and local governments to keep the builders at work. Schools were a mainstay for Marr & Holman—the firm did six in the 1930s. Courthouses at Union City, Jackson, Ripley, Dresden, Savannah, Byrdstown, and Gallatin as well as the Tennessee Supreme Court Building (fig. 36) also kept Marr & Holman from crashing.

Marr died in 1936, and Holman became the principal. The work of the firm from the 1940s and 1950s is not generally considered as architecturally significant as their projects of the 1920s and 1930s. When Holman died in 1952, the business passed to his sons who were not architects. The firm finally closed its doors in 1963.

Fig. 36. Marr & Holman, Architects, *Tennessee Supreme Court Building*, Nashville, 1937. **Designed in the same stripped classical style as the Nashville Post Office, this extremely formal and dignified building is classical in its proportions and symmetry but is simplified in its ornament except for the richly detailed cornice. The transitional nature of the Supreme Court's architecture—classicism on the way to modern—is particularly evident in the vivid Art Deco interior. The New Deal's Public Works Administration contributed $192,857 to the construction budget, with the remaining $450,000 financed by state bonds.**

Nashville and Postal History

The Post Office Department . . . is the delicate ear trumpet through which alike nations and families and isolated individuals whisper their joys and their sorrows, their convictions and their sympathies, to all who listen for their coming.

—Postmaster General Joseph Holt, *Annual Report*, 1859, quoted in U.S. Postal Service, *History of the United States Postal Service*, 28

The tender sensibilities of the Victorian postmaster were nowhere in evidence in the environs of Nashville's Public Square, when the city's first post office was established. In 1796, a little less than seventeen years after the establishment of Fort Nashborough and two months before Tennessee was admitted to the union, John Gordon was appointed the postmaster of Nashville. People passed their letters through Gordon's store—commonly believed to be of log construction—on the south side of the square across the street from the site of what is now the Metro Courthouse.[59]

Using commercial establishments as post offices was the tradition in early American history. In 1639 the first official notice of a postal service in the colonies designated a tavern in Boston as the repository of mail brought from or sent overseas, in line with the practice in England of using coffeehouses and taverns as mail drops.

Postal business was often an unprofitable sideline. But postmasters were entrepreneurs and handling mail was good for business. People who came to drop off or pick up letters often turned into customers for the goods on the surrounding shelves. America's Founding Entrepreneur, Benjamin Franklin, secured the postmastership of Philadelphia in 1737, when the thirty-one-year-old was a struggling

printer and publisher, and subsequently served as joint postmaster for the Crown from 1753. Franklin used his post office to sell his books, pamphlets, and newspapers, to send his publications through the mail to subscribers, and to establish a news network that supplied him with tips and copy.

During Franklin's tenure, the pragmatic businessman also effected many general improvements in postal service. He surveyed post offices and post roads as far south as Virginia, had milestones placed on principal roads, and laid out new and shorter routes, establishing the system of mileage from town to town as measured from post office to post office (now measured from city limit to city limit). Franklin organized weekly service from Philadelphia to Boston by means of relay riders. After the colonies began to separate from the colonizer, the Continental Congress named Franklin its first postmaster general in 1775, at a salary of $1,000 a year.[60]

The first mails came to Nashville by mounted courier from Washington and Philadelphia. The route the post riders traveled was arduous—from Washington to Abingdon, Virginia, then through Tennessee via Bristol, Knoxville, and Emory Gap, crossing the Cumberland River near Carthage, then following a trail to Hartsville, Castalian Springs, and Gallatin, before crossing the Cumberland again by the Nashville ferry.[61]

Mail traveled to the southwest territories by riverboat, until improvements to the Natchez Trace transformed Nashville from a stop along the way into a postal hub. In 1801 President Thomas Jefferson established the Trace—a footpath that for centuries had borne the imprint of buffalo and Native American—as a post road. Jefferson's action made the trail eligible for government funding, a key to riches that steamboat owners and railroad magnates would subsequently seize. Jefferson's postmaster general, Gideon Granger, suggested using troops stationed in the area "to clear out a wagon road and bridge the creeks and causeways between Nashville and Natchez." Granger noted that using the military to improve the post road would benefit the commerce of the entire Mississippi region. Once trail became road, couriers left Nashville every Saturday night, carrying mail to Natchez and on to New Orleans. Equally important, the Trace became the land avenue of goods flowing into the region from the river ports, in the days before steamships made navigation up the Mississippi possible.[62]

The first postal rates were calculated by distance: 6 cents for 30 miles, 10 cents for 100 miles, 25 cents for 350 miles. Because there were no stamps until the presidential administration of Tennessee's James K. Polk, the charges were often assessed on delivery. Nashville newspapers frequently carried lists of postal customers who had outstanding accounts of postage due.[63]

In 1823 all steamboat routes in the United States were designated as post roads, and in 1838 Congress followed suit with the railroad lines. These modes of transportation not only brought the mails to Nashville, they brought goods and services that made the city the commercial center of the Upper South. In unwelcome recognition of this status, Union troops occupied Nashville in 1862 and turned it into the supply depot for the Civil War's western front.[64]

President Rutherford B. Hayes used the construction of the Nashville Custom House, Courthouse, and Post Office to make the city a symbol of Reconstruction. Presidents Hoover and Roosevelt built the 1934 post office as a symbol of a powerful federal intervention. Throughout our history, then, the post office has served as the tie that binds Nashville to the rest of the nation. But bonds are ultimately forged by people. In the case of the U.S. Postal System, those people are the politicians who manipulated the system as a patronage trough, the postal workers who served it, and the customers who used it.

POLITICS AND PATRONAGE

The post office "is a source of boundless patronage to the executive, jobbing to the members of Congress and their friends, and [a] boundless abyss of public money."

—Thomas Jefferson, letter to James Madison, 1796, quoted in Craig et al., *The Federal Presence*, 164

Until 1971, when the Postal Reorganization Act went into effect, the Post Office Department and partisan politics enjoyed a symbiotic relationship. Article IX of the Articles of Confederation, a precursor to the Constitution ratified in 1781, gave Congress the sole right to establish and regulate the postal service, setting rates and approving postmasters. The 1792 Postal Act gave Congress the ability to create postal routes, which the members used as an expansionist tool, funding the laying or improving of post roads that carried not only the mails but settlers and goods, and discounting rates for newspapers to keep the hinterlands informed.

In 1829, under President Andrew Jackson, William Barry of Kentucky became the first postmaster general to sit as a member of the president's Cabinet. According to postal historian James Bruns, "Under Jackson and his loyal Postmaster General, the postal service became an integral part of the political machine, the principal patronage-dispensing agency for the party in power."[65]

The president, with the confirmation of the Senate, appointed not only the postmaster general but all postmasters in the United States except for the smallest post systems, which were handled by the postmaster general. Selections for postmasters were made by congressmen under a complicated "advisor" system requiring a candidate to gain the support of his or her representative and senator. Once rural free delivery came into being in 1896, the president and Senate had their say about rural mail carriers, too.[66]

In the early years of the Nashville postal system, the roster of postmasters included many of the family names that adorn prominent headstones in the city's cemeteries:

Cheatham, Lindsley, Wills, Cheney, Currey. The role of postmaster was a plum position, in part because it was not a full-time occupation. Robert Brownlee Currey, who served as Nashville postmaster from 1811 to 1826, also served as the city's mayor and ran a tavern simultaneously.

Currey's period of service was long for the era, because he had the backing of Tennessee politicians Sam Houston and Andrew Jackson. Houston even once fought a duel to keep Currey in office. John Quincy Adams had defeated Jackson in the presidential election of 1824 and appointed a member of his own Whig party to take over the Nashville post in 1826. Houston publicly labeled the new appointee a scoundrel, and shots were fired, to no avail. The Whig became postmaster, and Currey was out.[67]

The rivalry between political parties explains the noticeable in-and-out-and-in-again phenomenon in the roll call of Nashville postmasters. Whoever won the presidential election put postmasters of his political persuasion into office. The discarded postmasters waited in the wings, assuming their titles again when their party turned the tables.

Sometimes the connection was personal as well as political. Nashville postmaster Herman Hasslock, who served from 1874 to 1877, received his appointment from President Ulysses S. Grant because of a favor he had done for Grant when the two lived in Illinois. Legend has it that Grant's wagon broke down in front of Hasslock's house, and Hasslock supplied the future president with a new wheel. Grant told Hasslock to call on him if the Good Samaritan ever needed a favor. Years later Grant was president, Hasslock was living in Nashville, and the local postmastership came open. Hasslock asked for, and got, the job.[68]

With wagon wheels as job credentials, it is no wonder that the arteries of the postal system became increasingly clogged. The Chicago post office ground to a virtual halt in 1966 under a logjam of mail. Negotiations between the government and the seven labor unions representing various types of postal workers had devolved into an apparently endless series of accusations and recriminations. In congressional hearings over the sad state of postal affairs,

President Johnson's postmaster general, Lawrence O'Brien, admitted that "no human being can efficiently manage the nation's postal service as it is now constituted."[69] O'Brien had no control over workloads, pay scales, or postal rates, a condition unthinkable for the head of a private corporation.

In 1969 President Richard Nixon and his postmaster general, Winton "Red" Blount, decided that Congress should not be running the post office. They pushed through reforming legislation to make the system run more like a business. Key provisions of Title 39 of the U.S. Code included:

> Operational authority vested in a Board of Governors and Postal Service executive management rather than in Congress;
> Authority to issue public bonds to finance postal buildings and mechanization;
> Direct collective bargaining between management and employees;
> A rate-setting procedure built around an independent Postal Rate Commission.

The newly organized United States Postal Service began operating on July 1, 1971, as a self-supporting corporation wholly owned by the federal government.

UNEQUAL RIGHTS

> *Wanted: Young, skinny, wiry fellows not over 18. Must be expert riders willing to risk death daily. Orphans preferred.*
>
> —Postmaster General William H. Russell, newspaper advertisement for pony express riders, March 1860, from U.S. Postal Service, *History of the United States Postal Service*, 9

Juanita Johnson did not have to risk death to earn her pay at the Nashville Post Office. But she did have to face the obstacles of gender and racial politics in the 1960s to get a postal job, and to keep it. The post office could be a hostile place for clerks who had the education and skills to do the work but were the wrong sex and/or race.

She was Juanita Threalkill when she read in a 1959 Nashville newspaper that the civil service examination for postal clerks had been opened up to women. Threalkill took the exam and passed it, and then heard nothing for three years. "It was like I'd fallen off the map," she says.

But in 1962 Threalkill received a phone call asking her to report for the 2 A.M. night shift—it was the Christmas rush. She worked for two nights, cutting open bundles of mail and sorting the letters into trays, and then was told she was no longer needed. Threalkill was subsequently approached by postal worker Robert Everett, who asked if she would be willing to file a lawsuit against the Post Office Department based on gender discrimination. Everett was president of the local chapter of the National Alliance of Postal and Federal Employees, an organization founded in Chattanooga in 1913 (fig. 37), which Threalkill describes as "the NAACP of the postal service. I agreed to the lawsuit, but I did not realize the implications—that I was suing the U.S. government," she explains. "I just wanted a job to support my family."

To prove beyond a reasonable doubt that Threalkill was qualified for a postal position, Everett advised her to take the civil service exam every time it was offered, even though she had already taken it and passed. "The NAPFE would meet at Robert's house, or sometimes at Fisk or the library," Threalkill says. "Robert would coach me on the exam, which included a lot of math, reading interpretation, formulas— it was like a college entrance exam. I kept passing, but I got mighty sick of that test. Avon Williams [Nashville attorney and civil rights leader] was representing me. He wrote letters to President Johnson and Vice President Humphrey and Senator Albert Gore, Sr."

In 1966 Threalkill saw a photo in a local newspaper featuring two women—one white, one black—who had been hired as postal clerks, and "I realized that I had been passed over because I had filed the discrimination suit," she says. "That hurt my feelings so bad. This region just didn't want to hire women, and they especially didn't want to hire me." Finally, after more letters and legal maneuverings, the order came down from Atlanta. "I had to be put at the top of the federal register—no one else could be hired until

Fig. 37. National Alliance of Postal and Federal Employees, Executive Board, Juanita Threalkill, secretary, front row left, 1960s.

they hired me. On June 22, 1966, I got a letter telling me to report to work, and that is a letter I treasure. That was a glorious day."

Up to this point Threalkill had viewed her case as one of sex discrimination. Now she saw her race come into play. The managers at the post office "let me alone at first, until they realized that I wasn't going to blow my scheme exams." Threalkill was assigned to outgoing mail, which at that pre–Zip Code time utilized a system called "schemes" to sort mail. Mail was divided by states, then by regional and sectional centers, and then by towns.

"To learn the scheme for one of my states, Missouri, I had to memorize four to five hundred cards and where to place them [in the grid of slots]. I can still see those cards to this day," Threalkill laughs. "We called the scheme examination room the torture chamber. The examiner would hand you a hundred cards at random and you had to put them into the right slots almost without looking. You couldn't miss more than five and pass. I never missed a scheme because I

CHEEP CHARLIE

Charles J. Elder, the sage of Elder's Book Store, knows the politics and labor struggles, the inefficiencies and oddities, of old-time postal service from 30 years of firsthand experience. Elder worked at various positions in the Nashville postal system from 1943 to 1973. He says his wife tricked him into a position at the Broadway post office—ascertaining his willingness to work there when she knew that he had been offered a position and he did not. But Elder admits that working with the mail was in his genes.

According to Elder, the first post office in Tennessee—1794 in Rocky Mount—was run by his ancestor Will Cobb. In 1818 another forebear, one Joshua Elder, was postmaster in Clarksville. And his father was postmaster in Winchester in 1900. "So I guess you could say it runs in the family," he laughs.

Elder processed all the money orders for the region from his office on the second floor of the downtown post office, a task that qualified him to keep a gun in his desk drawer—"Guns were everywhere; everyone who handled money had one," he recalls— and also made him an object of suspicion when the ledgers failed to balance. He says that, unbeknownst to him, postal inspectors once watched him for months through slits in the surveillance corridors hidden in the post office walls, before discovering that some other clerk was robbing the till.

Because poultry shipped C.O.D. was Elder's responsibility, most of the downtown postal workers knew him by a nickname. "The chickens would arrive around 9 o'clock, and often it was cold, and the little guys would be cheeping," Elder says. "One of the workers would call out, 'Cheep, cheep, Charlie, cheep, cheep.' So then everyone called me Cheep Charlie. A lot of stuff you'd never think of came through the mails in those days," Elder says, "and people would call for their chickens, or shrubs, or rose bushes, right at the windows in the lobby."

Elder expresses a healthy skepticism about postal policies that required an armed guard to shepherd all registered mail moving through the overpass between the train station and the post office, while he was left to his own defenses while carrying thousands of dollars along lonely roads. "They used to send me out by myself in an Army jeep with the paychecks for the soldiers on maneuvers at Cedars of Lebanon Park—George Patton drilled the troops there for a while. I'd exchange their checks for money orders that the soldiers would then mail to their families. Sometimes I'd return

with as much as $12,000, but I never had a guard to protect me," he shrugs.

Elder had direct experience with the patronage system that clogged upward advancement in the postal system. "Who got the jobs was full of politics—it stunk," he recalls. "I passed one examination for a position five times, and with the highest score, but I couldn't get the job, because the postmaster had a buddy who wanted it. And [the postmaster] resented that I'd done so well on the test. Sometimes the boss made me work just late enough at night to miss the last trolley home, and I had to walk six miles." Postal work was a means to literary ends for Elder, who had previously served as a researcher and writer for the Work Projects Administration *Guide to Tennessee* in the 1930s. "At the post office I could make a living, but I wanted to be a writer, and I had the bookstore," Elder says. "My wife managed the store while I was at the post office. After I got off work, I'd take over. Gave me a good outlet for my surplus energy."

As a postal clerk, Elder is proudest of his role in developing the American Postal Workers Union, for which he served as national legislative liaison for decades. It was hard to get the post office to accept the union, especially in the 1950s, and even more especially in the South. Elder labored long and hard to organize the postal clerks, because wages frozen during World War II had risen little since then. "It took us 12 years after the war to get a raise, and I never earned more than 96 cents an hour while I was there," Elder says. (information from Charles J. Elder, interview by Christine Kreyling, March 3, 2000)

NEITHER SNOW, NOR RAIN, NOR HEAT, NOR GLOOM OF NIGHT . . .
BUT SOMETIMES BEES

Nelson Andrews:

"About 20, 25 years ago I started keeping bees (fig. 38) in my backyard on Warner Place. I'd ordered a batch of bees to establish a new hive. To start a hive takes approximately one-tenth the 65,000 in a hive that's really growing and going during the summer honey flow. So you buy those bees, and separately you buy a queen. They're shipped at the same time, but the queen comes in a little box all by herself.

"One Sunday afternoon in early April, I got a call from the downtown post office, telling me that my bees were loose. Bees are shipped in very sturdy packaging, but somehow the box had fallen off a conveyor belt and burst open. They'd had to close off the entire work area in the back, because the bees just took over. The superintendent said, 'You gotta come down here and get these bees.'

"So I got in my beekeeper suit, took some bee equipment, and drove down there. Now bees when they're pleasant make a low humming sound. But when they're angry, bees make a real tough sound, almost a roar. So I went into the post office workroom and could tell right away that these were angry bees, no doubt about it.

"I went back out to the super and said I didn't understand why they were so shook up. They'd been out awhile, and should have settled down. Found out that they'd done everything wrong. The super said that when the bees got loose, the postal workers tried to fight the bees, hit out at them. It's a natural impulse, but you cannot fight bees. Doesn't work, just makes 'em mad. All you can do is run. And one guy had tried to 'fix' the bees by spraying insecticide on them. So now we had 6,000 *really* mad bees.

"I told the super he had to let me find the box with the queen, to put her near the hive I'd brought, to round them up. Well, that was the worst thing I could have asked for. Nobody except postal employees is allowed to touch any of the packages. They must have debated for 30 or 40 minutes about suspending the bureaucratic rules. Finally they let me go through the packages, because I'd explained that, without the queen, the post office had bees until they all died of starvation. You can't grab 'em one at a time.

"Once I found the queen and got her into the hive, and all the bees understood; they went into the hive, and I closed it up and took them home.

"Shortly after, the postmaster called me and said that he thought they were going to have to stop shipping bees. I told him they could never do it, that the lobbyists would descend on him with a vengeance. You see, bees are just too important, they pollinate crops. You have to have bees, even if sometimes they shut down the post office for a whole afternoon." (Nelson Andrews, interview by Christine Kreyling, July 5, 2000)

Fig. 38. U.S. Postal Service, *Stamp with a Honeybee,* 1987. **Stamps that sting. The postal service has devoted two commemoratives to the honeybee, recognizing its vital role in American agriculture.**

THE MAIL FACTORY

Herbert Fox, former postal worker, and currently man-about-town as the editor of *Nfocus*:

"I worked at the downtown post office in the '40s, during World War II, for two Christmas vacations from Montgomery Bell Academy. My father got me the job, he knew someone.

"I remember working both Christmas Eves.

"I sorted mail going to other cities—part of the regional distribution system. The only machine was the one that stamped on the postmarks. I stood in the big workroom in the back—pretty bare-bones because the public never was allowed in there—and they brought the mail to my station in boxes. You had to memorize the slots into which the mail was sorted—I was like a trained chimpanzee.

"But it was a good Christmas job, and all the workers were very nice to me. Only sometimes I'd be overwhelmed by the sheer volume—the mail never ends. Then I'd feel like Lucy Ricardo in the candy factory." (Herbert Fox, interview by Christine Kreyling, April 13, 2000)

knew how to study for the test. I had watched my brother-in-law, who was a postal clerk, practice for his schemes. He'd take an empty Coca-Cola case, and he'd stay up all night, throwing his cards into it, over and over. That's what it took to pass," she says.

When her supervisors realized that Threalkill was not going to flunk out, some began a campaign of what she calls "subtle harassment." In one instance, she was shifted to a different floor to work at a job with which she was not familiar. She was placed at the end of a conveyor belt and told to handle the flow generated by four men throwing mail onto the belt. Supervisor Ray Handy stood and watched her. "Of course I got backed up—it was called 'getting stuck.' There were four of them and one of me and they knew the system and I'd never worked it before," Threalkill says. "This was considered unsatisfactory work."

Threalkill was also cited for clocking out at the wrong time clock. "We only had thirty minutes for lunch, and one day there was a long line at the time clock near my area. Someone said, 'Let's just go downstairs and clock out, or we'll lose eight or nine minutes.' Everybody did it. . . .

"But in October of 1967, I got two letters of warning—in the same envelope—for these incidents," Threalkill says. "I filed a grievance claiming unfair treatment that went into arbitration." It took two years for the case to be settled. The postal service removed from her personnel file the letter of warning for the first incident, but not the second.

"I swallowed a lot, because I was twenty-nine years old and had six children and I needed the job," Threalkill says. "Mr. Handy told me one day that he didn't like the way I walked, that I seemed to 'saunter,'" Threalkill recalls. "And if any white woman would stop by to say hello, Mr. Handy would come over and say that I was doing too much talking. All the white women eventually moved to office jobs, you could tell because they'd start wearing high heels. I stayed on the floor of the main post office for four years."

During those four years Threalkill remembers that "things got very weird" because of the civil rights protests in Nashville. "Stokely Carmichael came to town to give a speech, and the next day you could have cut the tension on the workroom floor with a knife. Whites stopped talking to blacks, or if they did, they didn't get promoted. You found out who your true friends were. This was the night shift, which we called the 'Klan shift' because people would sometimes say derogatory things. I ignored them, because it was based in ignorance," Threalkill says.

Threalkill eventually applied for a position at the postal station in North Nashville, where she remained for seven years. In 1977 a general clerk position opened up at the downtown post office. "This was a desk job, which made it a coveted one," Threalkill explains. "A white woman had been primed for the job by the union, but I took the test and passed it with a higher score. I got the job, because the system had finally changed. They couldn't just pick favorites anymore; they had to adhere to the process."[70]

In 1996 Juanita Johnson retired from the U.S. Postal Service. Until she was asked to review her memories by the Frist Center, Johnson says she never thought of herself as a pioneer, and had received no special recognition. It's about time.

PERSPECTIVE

EDC
TUCK HINTON EVERTON ARCHITECTS
901 BROADWAY

Fig. 39. Tuck Hinton Everton Architects, *Redevelopment Scheme for the Nashville Post Office*, 1989. Colored pencil and pastel on paper; 32 × 26½ in. Tuck Hinton Architects.

MOVING ON

In December 1986 the Nashville Post Office prepared for its last Christmas rush. Postal workers braced for the red-and-green onslaught—an estimated 57 million cards and letters from Middle Tennessee, enough to make a stack 20.6 miles high.[71] In the spring of 1987 the Broadway post office became a mere local station, and the central postal distribution operations moved to an industrial park near the airport. Planes had replaced trains as the means for moving the vast majority of mail from city to city. The site next to Union Station was no longer an attraction but a handicap.

The new building on Royal Parkway would not be a major federal monument in Nashville. That was clear right from the beginning in the language used to promote it. The "General Mail Facility" would by design be a "mail factory," in the words of Postmaster David Huggins. The U.S. Postal Service of the 1980s had entirely different practical as well as symbolic needs from those of the federal government in 1934. With a 253,000-square-foot footprint—almost five acres—the one-story structure on its 25-acre tract would be a Mail Mall, able to accommodate the 1,200 workers and the mail-handling and bar-code–reading machines required to process the daily haul of 2.5 million pieces of mail—94 percent of it business mail. To provide the service Americans had come to expect in their consumer affairs, the new facility would be open 24 hours a day, 7 days a week.[72]

Former Postmaster General Marvin Runyon explains the new philosophy behind post office architecture as swimming in the mainstream of commerce rather than Big Brother making a splash. "The downtown post office is very imposing. A new post office doesn't need to be a big government building. It should look like it can compete in the marketplace and people should feel comfortable using it," Runyon says.[73]

The question was, what to do with the old shrine to federalism? In June 1988 the postal service advertised for redevelopment proposals for the building. The idea was to retain a much smaller postal operation on the main floor and surrender the rest of the vast space to private office use.[74]

In 1989 the EDC development company was hired to hawk the post office building. President Pat Emery released schematic drawings by Tuck Hinton Everton Architects that showed a nineteen-story office tower looming over the 1934 building like the proverbial eight-hundred-pound gorilla, dwarfing the tower of Union Station (fig. 39). The retention of the style of the original post office for the much more massive "addition"—theoretically admirable as a gesture of historical respect—unfortunately illustrated how "stripped classicism," when blown out of proportion, could result in an effect reminiscent of fascist architecture of the 1930s.

In an interview with *Nashville Banner* reporter Mary Hance, Emery predicted that the redevelopment proposal would be "a 1992 project," noting that "three new office towers are already in the works for downtown."[75] Fortunately for Nashville's architectural history, the bottom fell out of the office market before the scheme could be realized.

When in 1996 The Frist Foundation proposed installing a visual arts center in the downtown post office, Nashvillians recognized a compatible tenant, because the building's architecture recalls the classically inspired temples to the fine arts that other cities built long ago. Designed as a civic monument, the post office has adapted to a new civic purpose with the nonchalance that all fine old buildings are good at—absorbing the present moment into the larger context of history.

Fig. 40. *Door, with detail.* Cast aluminum; 84 × 36 in. Frist Center for the Visual Arts. **An icon that decorates several of the original aluminum interior doors of the building inspired the logo of the new Frist Center for the Visual Arts. Although its precise meaning is unclear, its intriguing forms are characteristic of the period. The same motif or variants of it appeared in other Art Deco buildings across the United States.**

History of the Frist Center
for the Visual Arts

Keel Hunt and the Staff of the Frist Center for the Visual Arts

The origins of the Frist Center can be traced to a myriad of sources all over the Nashville community:

> In dozens of neighborhood discussions citywide;
> In the hopes of teachers for their young students;
> In the imaginations of children.

The Frist Center for the Visual Arts is a reality today because Nashvillians and their community leaders shared a strong and compelling vision: they believed their city could, and should, become a cultural center where children and adults could see, firsthand, superb exhibitions representing the world's greatest art.

Over time, through much hard work by many hands, the landmark Broadway Post Office (fig. 40) has been brought into city ownership, its historical significance preserved. It has been given new life as a vibrant institution to benefit the citizens of Nashville and its visitors.

Nashville's need for a major visual arts facility in the downtown area had been a topic of lively discussion for more than thirty years. Since 1969, as many as seventeen studies and reports by private and governmental institutions had made reference to the lack in Nashville of adequate art exhibition facilities in a central, generally accessible location. Although nothing more was done, primarily because of the want of major financial support for the project, the need for such a facility continued to grow.

Then, in 1993, an extraordinary public process called "Nashville's Agenda" drew thousands of citizens into discussions citywide about the future of Tennessee's capital city. This community goal-setting process produced a report in January 1994 identifying twenty-one goals for "making Nashville the best it can be," specifically including an ambitious goal for the "Arts":

> Nashville should be a cultural center with excellent facilities for the visual and performing arts and diverse opportunities accessible to all Nashvillians and visitors alike.

A related objective for "Downtown Development" was even more explicit:

> Develop a museum or a major tourist/cultural attraction downtown.

This grand vision—generated by an unprecedented, broad, citizen-based process—led to concrete action in March 1994. The Steering Committee for "Nashville's Agenda" appointed an "Action Team for the Arts" to help move the city closer to the new goal for the arts. Chaired by Kenneth L. Roberts, President of The Frist Foundation, the team was a broad and diverse group.

Over an eighteen-month period, this group of volunteers reviewed all the earlier studies, visited all local art museums and university galleries, studied the space needs and plans of art institutions in Nashville, and visited art museums and galleries in other major cities around the country. The team also commissioned new demographic and marketing research on the arts in Nashville and hosted two public forums. All confirmed the need for a visual arts center in downtown Nashville. It was clear that, in addition to the educational benefits that would be provided by such a center, the citizens of Nashville would also derive significant tourism and other economic benefits from the attraction of such a facility.

The Action Team reported this recommendation: A new kind of institution should be created in Nashville to provide world-class visual arts exhibition facilities for the general public and enhance the education of schoolchildren and families. It would have no permanent collection but instead would accommodate art exhibitions of national and international scope, as well as the works of local and regional artists.

But where? An additional marketing survey in 1995 gave strong indication that Nashvillians would support such a unique art center, and the same study showed that the neighborhood of the Broadway Post Office and Union Station would be a preferred location because of historic character, accessibility, and convenience. The Frist Foundation then commissioned LORD Cultural Resources Planning & Management Inc. of Toronto, Canada—a leading museum consulting firm—to undertake a feasibility analysis for the proposed Visual Arts Center. The LORD organization affirmed that the former Main Post Office itself would be the perfect place. Renovating the old post office building was deemed to be more cost-effective than any other alternative, and such a project could preserve this historically significant Art Deco structure for the enjoyment of future generations.

These planning steps combined to set in motion an extraordinary sequence of breakthrough developments that created the Frist Center for the Visual Arts:

◙ After lengthy discussions between representatives of The Frist Foundation and officials of the U.S. Postal Service, the Postal Service, under Postmaster General Marvin Runyon (1992–98), agreed to convey the Broadway property for $4.4 million, on condition that it would be used solely for a visual arts center and only if the Postal Service were allowed to retain a customer service center in the lower level of the building.

◙ An agreement was reached whereby Nashville's Metropolitan Government, under the leadership of Mayor Philip Bredesen (1991–99) and with the overwhelming support of the Metropolitan Council, would purchase the building. As the new owner, the Metropolitan Development and Housing Agency provided funds for the basic renovation of the historic property in accordance with the highest-quality museum standards. The public costs to acquire and renovate the building were "capped" at $19.9 million. The building is presently leased to the Center under a 99-year lease. Metro Nashville has no further financial obligation with respect to the Center.

◙ The Frist Foundation and the family of Dr. Thomas F. Frist, Jr., pledged at least $25 million to the project. These funds provided for all additional costs necessary to renovate the building into a world-class facility and to initiate an operating endowment for the center.

◙ A new Visual Arts Center Foundation was created by The Frist Foundation to provide necessary future financial support.

◙ A 22-person founding Board of Trustees for the Frist Center was created and is composed of a broad and diverse group of community leaders, including working artists and educators, as well as representatives from the civic and business communities and government.

◙ The Board of the Frist Center, after conducting a national search for a professional museum executive, announced in December 1998 that Chase W. Rynd, then the highly praised Executive Director of the Tacoma Art Museum, would become the founding Executive Director and CEO of the Frist Center for the Visual Arts. Rynd assumed his responsibilities in February 1999 and proceeded to develop an outstanding and distinguished staff.

◙ During 1999 and 2000, under the guidance of the Board and staff, detailed planning for the operation of the new Center took place and the building underwent renovations.

◙ Additionally, an entire city block behind the post office building was acquired separately and has been redeveloped into a beautiful parklike area, which will provide some parking and greater accessibility to the Center.

■ The U.S. Postal Service completed its new retail facility on the lower level and opened to the public in November 1999.

■ The Frist Center opened to the public on April 8, 2001.

In addition to being a striking facility with dynamic educational programs and a commitment to exhibiting world-class art, this unique institution also represents an inspiring case study in public-private collaboration for the benefit of the entire community.

Because of this special history, the Frist Center today is a unique civic institution in many ways. Its unique combination of activities is grounded in the institutional Mission of the Frist Center, as well as in its policy mandates (see pp. 14–15), with the following areas of strong emphasis.

EDUCATION

While the Center provides opportunities for learners of all ages to become actively engaged, the primary beneficiaries of the Center's educational efforts are Nashville's school-aged children—with programs and outreach focused strongly on children and their families. The Center's commitment to young people is also reflected in the policy that all visitors 18 and under are admitted free of charge, providing them access to a "window on the world" of art. School programs are exhibition-based and support the curriculum content identified by the school system. They reflect the input of classroom teachers and educators from across the community.

OUTREACH

The Center's extensive outreach programs are designed to reach the varied segments of the Nashville community. Plans are being developed in cooperation with a broad segment of youth and family service providers, local community centers, the parks system, the Nashville Public Library, and other community leaders in order to encourage nontraditional audiences to visit the Center.

LOCAL COLLABORATION

From the very beginning of planning for the Frist Center, there have been extensive consultation and collaboration with other art and cultural institutions in the Nashville area, as well as with collectors and artists in the community. The Frist Center promotes awareness of the exhibitions and programs offered by neighboring institutions, including Belle Meade Plantation, Belmont Mansion, Cheekwood—Tennessee Botanical Gardens and Museum of Art, the Country Music Foundation, Fisk University Galleries, The Hermitage: Home of Andrew Jackson, the Nashville Public Library, The Parthenon, the Tennessee State Museum, and Vanderbilt University Fine Arts Gallery, among others. It also joins with other local cultural and arts institutions on interdisciplinary programs and activities.

FACILITIES AND PROGRAMS

Unique also is the close integration of all elements of the Frist Center, from its physical plant to its extraordinarily varied activities. The state-of-the-art facility is designed to serve the Center's programs and further its core educational mission and mandates. Likewise, the Center's exhibition program is designed in conjunction with the Frist Center's facility, educational resources, and programs to help visitors of all ages better understand art and its makers. Short-term exhibitions, two to three months in duration, are housed in the over-10,000-square-foot Main Level exhibition gallery. Longer-term exhibitions of up to three years, in the 5,200-square-foot Upper Level gallery, enable visitors to return over time and allow community educators to integrate school-group tours and exhibition-related educational activities into their curricular planning more thoroughly. The Contemporary Artists Project (CAP) Gallery, adjacent to the Main Level exhibition gallery, underlines the Frist Center's support for the creativity of living artists. Opposite the CAP Gallery, the Education Gallery explores ideas and themes related to the content of ongoing exhibitions. The Community Arts Gallery, on the west side of the Main Level, is devoted to exhibitions of local interest and related to the Center's outreach in the community.

Next to the Upper Level exhibition galleries, the ArtQuest Gallery, a pioneering 4,000-square-foot interactive educational space, encourages the visitor to gain enduring understandings of the basic principles of art and visual looking skills through hands-on opportunity and computer programs, all closely coordinated with the Center's exhibition programs. The Media and Technology Resource Center, on the same level, offers media and printed resources for visitors and educators who would like to learn more about the works in the exhibitions. Three classrooms—one a computer lab—also support the educational programs. On the Main Level are an Orientation Gallery, which acquaints visitors with the exhibitions and programs of the Frist Center and other Nashville arts organizations, and a 250-seat auditorium.

EXHIBITIONS

In April 2000, to unanimous public acclaim and excitement, the Frist Center for the Visual Arts announced the schedule for its first year of exhibitions. An exceptional array of art— ranging from pre-Columbian ceramics and exquisitely illuminated medieval manuscripts to paintings by renowned European and American masters—would inaugurate an ambitious long-range exhibition program designed to bring the world's finest art to Nashville. Coming from international, U.S., and local sources, both public and private, and covering a variety of artistic disciplines, styles, periods, and cultural contexts, the majority of the works had never before been displayed in Nashville. Those on loan from the rich collections of local partner institutions could now be appreciated in a new context.

Five exhibitions, all exclusively sponsored through the generosity of AmSouth, launched the grand opening of the Frist Center for the Visual Arts on April 8, 2001. From one of North America's most celebrated art museums, "European Masterworks: Paintings from the Collection of the Art Gallery of Ontario" features ninety-five works surveying close to

six hundred years of painting by many of Europe's finest masters. Organized specifically for the Frist Center's grand opening in cooperation with the Art Gallery of Ontario, Toronto, the exhibition is on view in the Center's Main Level exhibition gallery until July 8, 2001.

In the Upper Level gallery, "An Enduring Legacy: Art of the Americas from Nashville Collections" celebrates art in North, Central, and South America from the pre-Columbian and ancient Native American periods through 1980. Generous loans from Nashville public and private collections of more than 140 important works make up this yearlong presentation. Its broad range—from painting to sculpture, ceramics, furniture, and industrial design—mirrors the great breadth of art that the Center's future exhibitions will explore.

The third opening exhibition, "From Post Office to Art Center: A Nashville Landmark in Transition," the subject of this book, examines the history of the Frist Center's Art Deco–style building on Broadway in downtown Nashville and the founding of the Frist Center for the Visual Arts. It fills the Center's Community Arts Gallery until early 2002.

The Contemporary Artists Project (CAP) Gallery hosts two exhibitions in 2001, each approximately four months long. The opening exhibition features a sculptural tableau, The Administrator, by Nashville artist Michael Aurbach, a humorous commentary on secrecy and the exercise of power by people in positions of authority. The Education Gallery features work by participants in the Center's Community Outreach programs in response to the "European Masterworks" exhibition.

Following the close of "European Masterworks," the Main Level exhibition gallery hosts a major national traveling exhibition from July 20 to September 9, 2001. "Modernism & Abstraction: Treasures from the Smithsonian American Art Museum" is one of eight exhibitions in Treasures to Go, from the Smithsonian American Art Museum, touring the nation through 2002. Subsequently, two complementary exhibitions open on the Main Level on September 27, 2001. "Realms of Faith: Medieval and Byzantine Art from the

Walters Art Museum, Baltimore" presents one hundred precious religious and secular objects in a variety of media. Organized by the Walters Art Museum, Baltimore, exclusively for the Frist Center, it closes January 13, 2002. Concurrently, "Leaves of Gold: Treasures of Manuscript Illumination from Philadelphia Collections" includes some eighty illuminations, many still in their original manuscripts. "Leaves of Gold," which closes January 6, 2002, is organized by the Philadelphia Museum of Art in association with the Philadelphia Area Consortium of Special Collections Libraries and with the support of the Philadelphia Exhibitions Initiative. The second contemporary exhibition in the CAP Gallery will feature work by New York artist Petah Coyne from September 18, 2001, to January 13, 2002.

RECYCLING THE NASHVILLE POST OFFICE   *Christine Kreyling*

Facts as facts do not always create a spirit of reality, because reality is a spirit.

—G. K. Chesterton, *Come to Think of It*, 1930

When the team of federal and local architects designed the Nashville Post Office as an imposing monument to government, they knew that reality is largely a matter of perception. Seab A. Tuck III, the principal architect of the Frist Center for the Visual Arts renovation, had to work with the obvious strengths of the 1934 building while subtly shifting the perception to the new reality of a visual arts center (fig. 41).

"You start with a building that's very hierarchical and stable in character," Tuck explains. "That kind of architectural message did not convey the Frist Center's mission, which is populist, educational, fun." Tuck, a partner in the Nashville firm of Tuck Hinton Architects, democratized the structure by opening up strong sight lines and predictable avenues through the building via the Community Arts Gallery and by incorporating transparency with the glass-walled central gallery stairs and bridges. "Originally everything behind the lobby was closed to the public. Now the whole building is a civic center. The new stairs and bridges allow people to see others moving through the public spaces."

But if the post office's image needed tweaking, the building was nevertheless a well-made vessel into which the new meaning of the Frist Center could be poured. "You couldn't make this building today for less than $60 million, just the shell," Tuck says, "and it's perfect for art. You need a big box with tall ceilings, broad column spacings, a large freight elevator, a big loading and unloading capacity. Well, here it is, sitting right at the edge of downtown, with good access to the interstate. Besides, you're getting three for one because you're creating a visual arts center, renovating a Nashville landmark, and making an energy center for downtown that can stimulate other redevelopment."

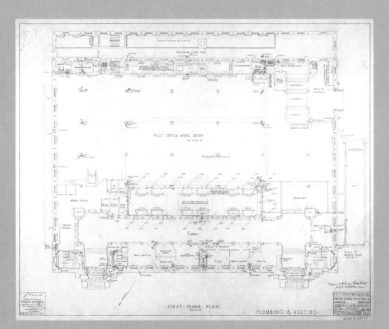

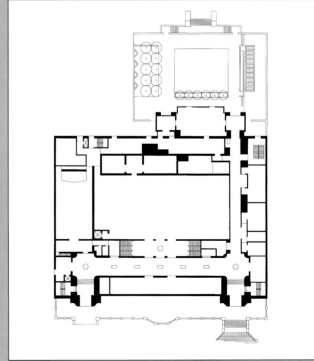

Fig. 41. Marr & Holman, Architects, *Ground Plan of the Nashville Post Office*. Ink on linen; 31 × 39 in. Metropolitan Development and Housing Agency, on deposit with the Frist Center for the Visual Arts. Compared with Tuck Hinton Architects, *Ground Plan of the Frist Center for the Visual Arts*.

For years Nashville developers debated proposals for revitalizing the area around the Gulch—office towers, festival retail, the downtown library, and the Farmers' Market all put in an appearance. Now, with the advent of the Frist Center—as well as the adaptive reuse of Cummins Station and the Union Station baggage building, the transformation of Braid Electric into the mixed-use 1100 Demonbreun Building, the construction of the MTA landport, the reconstruction of Demonbreun Street west of the Gulch, the plans to preserve the Demonbreun viaduct, and the new Gulch Master Plan to create an urban neighborhood in the former railroad corridor—the Union Station Hotel is no longer a lone voice crying in a decaying wilderness. And the Metropolitan Development and Housing Agency—recognizing the Frist Center as the much-needed anchor tenant it had been looking for—in 1998 established the Arts Center Redevelopment District, to provide infrastructure improvements and tax incentives to encourage further initiatives.

To make the post office work for art, Tuck faced two basic structural challenges. "The placement of the auditorium meant that we had to cut out three 24-foot load-bearing columns that had supported the floor of the second level and hang that floor from the roof above via six steel beams. And we had to move the freight elevator—large enough to drive a car into—to make a 'crossroad' through the building to the front lobby. You see, the idea of having a major entrance in what was the rear of the building wasn't in the original scheme. At first, there was no café on the south side, with its glass pavilion overlooking the granite-walled courtyard. There was just a parking lot," Tuck says.

But the design team quickly realized that where the cars are is where the vast majority of people come from, and that making visitors walk around the sides of the building to the Broadway facade not only would be inefficient but would undercut the welcoming aspect the architects were trying to establish. So they created an equally strong entrance on the south facade, with fountains by local glass artist Tom Fuhrman and a grassy courtyard, to embrace the area lying south of Broadway. This reorientation helps to spread patrons throughout the building, further diminishing the sense of hierarchy of the original layout.

To make sure that the design team included the educational, art handling, administrative, and retail configurations—and the up-to-the-minute technologies—necessary to support the galleries, Tuck enlisted an army of consultants. "The architect is the orchestrater of a building project, the one who looks at the big picture. But to fine-tune all the details, you have to surround yourself with experts," Tuck explains.

The integration of all these spaces respects the principle that sunlight is kind to people but not to artworks. Offices and classrooms, eating spaces and auditorium, gift shop and media resource center run along the building's windows, wrapping the art galleries that are literally and symbolically the heart of the Frist Center. Yet the interior is not a dark cave; south-facing clerestory windows flood the core with natural light. "There was originally an artificially illuminated skylight in the post office lobby, but that had been covered in 1959. We didn't want a skylight—natural or artificial—because of its potential to leak water into the art space. So we planned a clerestory to bring direct sunlight into the lobby and to reflect it indirectly into the rest of the people spaces," Tuck says.

Understandably, the color schemes in the galleries of the Frist Center will vary from exhibition to exhibition. In the lobby, however, the architects restored the use of saturated colors and silver much favored by Art Deco.

The result of all these design calculations, and the collective civic will to turn design into reality, is a new place of communal gathering in an old landmark. Today the Frist Center stands firmly on its 1934 foundations, a vital new institution supported by the solid structure of the past. (information from Seab A. Tuck III, interview by Christine Kreyling, July 7, 2000)

*The cornerstone will be laid November 4th. I have expressed my
belief that the stone should be checked to receive a copper box which
may contain articles customary for a ceremony of this kind.*

—Supervising Engineer H. W. Thayer, letter to the Office
of the Supervising Architect of the Treasury Department,
October 3, 1933

Thayer was referring to what we call a time capsule, a collection of
memorabilia that allows one era to speak to another across time.
The task for the architects and contractors of the renovation was to
unearth it. The idea was to put the historical documents on display
for the opening of the Frist Center. Artifacts from our millennial
age are to be interred in a new capsule under the Center's south
terrace. Sound simple? Anything but.

For starters the cornerstone is a block of marble 3½ feet high,
8 feet long, and 8 inches thick, weighing 2½ tons. Resting on top
of this massive stone are the large marble slabs of the building's
walls. Removing the cornerstone for examination could, therefore,
crack or otherwise damage the corner of the structure. Such an
operation is an issue of finesse rather than brute strength—like
removing a wedge of wedding cake from the lowest layer. You need
a strong knife and an adequate supporting surround to keep the
upper layers from cracking and chipping.

An interior avenue seemed simpler. "We thought that we could
approach the time capsule from inside the building, by removing
the marble walls and a radiator enclosure located in an intermediate landing of the corner stair, and then drilling into the stone,"
says Seab Tuck, principal architect for the renovation. "But we
realized on closer examination of the original construction drawings that the capsule could be located underneath the slab that
forms the stair landing. This would mean damaging the marble
floor of the landing." The architect did not want to proceed until
he knew exactly where the capsule was embedded.

For six months construction officials searched for the exact
location of the capsule, at one point even closing the block of
Broadway in front of the post office so the cornerstone could be
X-rayed. Contractors ultimately carved a tiny tunnel to the cornerstone from the interior stairwell, digging and chiseling through
2½ feet of brick wall. Finally, at 3:45 P.M. on September 11, 2000,
a stonemason emerged with the time-blackened copper box and
handed it to Chase Rynd, Executive Director of the Frist Center.

Inside the box, which measures 12 inches long by 6 inches tall
by 4 inches deep, Rynd and his staff discovered a curious collection of artifacts, including:

- a July 20, 1824, bank draft for $88.76 signed by "Major
General Andrew Jackson"

- a tour book of The Hermitage: Home of Andrew Jackson

- the *Postal Supervisor* magazine of October 1933 containing
a history of Nashville's postmasters

- a Nashville Chamber of Commerce tourism brochure

- a copy of President Roosevelt's "Reemployment Agreement," which contains a set of instructions for employers—
on child labor, hours in a work week, etc.—designed to
maximize the number of workers who could be employed
at a time when jobs were so scarce

- the first issue of the *Columbus Balbo Review,* an Italian-
American newsletter published in Birmingham, Alabama

- a 1933 publication called *The Nashville Jewish Community*

- an imperfect stamp featuring the logo of the 1933
"Century of Progress" exposition in Chicago

- special supplements to the *Tennessean* and the *Nashville
Banner* devoted to the Nashville Post Office and the history
of postal service in the city

- a small snapshot of 5-year-old Barbara Crumbecker,
annotated, "direct descendant of General Robert E. Lee."

While newspaper accounts of the cornerstone laying indicated that
a Bible was to be placed in the capsule, no copy of Holy Scripture
was found.

"We nearly gave up the search for the time capsule, but now
I'm really glad that we didn't," says Rynd. "I think our visitors
will be fascinated to see this odd-but-true assortment of historic
artifacts."

Case closed. (information from Seab A. Tuck III, interview by
Christine Kreyling, July 7, 2000, and Chase W. Rynd, interview by
Christine Kreyling, September 14, 2000)

Conceived as an idea and nurtured by an entire community, the Frist Center for the Visual Arts has become a reality through visionary leadership. Its foundations are solid: commitment to quality and dedication to community.

With the opening of the doors of the Frist Center for the Visual Arts, the process that led to its creation is complete. But the greatest challenge still lies ahead: ensuring that the Frist Center will enrich its visitors' lives for generations to come by joining and collaborating with all of Nashville's other cultural institutions as a center for education, reflection, and discussion.

Notes

1. Lois Craig et al., *The Federal Presence: Architecture, Politics, and Symbols in United States Government Building* (Cambridge, Mass.: MIT Press, 1978), xiii.
2. Ann Vines Reynolds, "Nashville's Custom House," *Tennessee Historical Quarterly* 37, no. 3 (fall 1978): 263.
3. James H. Bruns, *Great American Post Offices* (New York: John Wiley & Sons, 1998), 180.
4. Ibid., 81–82.
5. Susan Knowles, "A. C. Webb: Artist/Architect," Master's thesis, Vanderbilt University, 1986, 98.
6. George Howe, quoted in Richard Guy Wilson, Dianne H. Pilgrim, and Dickran Tashjian, *The Machine Age in America, 1918–1941*, exh. cat. (New York: The Brooklyn Museum, 1986), 149.
7. Bruns, *Great American Post Offices*, 94.
8. Ibid.
9. Don H. Doyle, *Nashville since the 1920s* (Knoxville: University of Tennessee Press, 1985), 85–86.
10. "Big Building Year for City," *Nashville Banner*, December 29, 1929, 1.
11. "Publix Theater Officials Here," *Nashville Banner*, October 23, 1930, 1.
12. Doyle, *Nashville since the 1920s*, 85–86.
13. T. W. Naylor and E. R. Martin, *Nashville, Tennessee: Investigation in the Formulation of a Public Buildings' Program*, case no. 176,031-C, Treasury Department Papers, Record Group 121, National Archives, Washington, D.C., 3–4.
14. S. Lowman, TMS (typed manuscript signed), "Advertisement for Federal Building Site," March 7, 1931, Records of the Public Building Service, Record Group 121, National Archives, Washington, D.C.
15. U.S. Postal Service, *History of the United States Postal Service, 1775–1993* (Washington, D.C.: U.S. Postal Service, 1993), 11.
16. Ferry K. Heath to Senator Kenneth McKellar, typed letter (hereafter TL) (copy), August 19, 1931, Records of the Public Building Service, Record Group 121, National Archives, Washington, D.C.
17. Kay Beasely, "Hub of Wartime Transportation," *Nashville Banner*, October 15, 1986.

18. A. W. Mellon, Secretary of the Treasury, to the Honorable Attorney General, TL (copy), December 3, 1931, Treasury Department Papers, Record Group 121, National Archives, Washington, D.C.
19. Hallum W. Goodloe to Ogden L. Mills, typed letter signed (hereafter TLS), April 9, 1932, Record Group 121, National Archives, Washington, D.C.
20. The above facts are from Treasury Department Papers, Record Group 121, National Archives, Washington, D.C., passim.
21. Antoinette Lee, *Architects to the Nation: The Rise and Decline of the Supervising Architect's Office* (New York: Oxford University Press, 2000), 85–124.
22. Quoted in Henry-Russell Hitchcock and Philip Johnson, *The International Style* (New York: W. W. Norton & Company, 1966), 13–14.
23. Edwin B. Morris, *Federal Architect* 1, no. 1 (July 1930): 4.
24. Craig et al., *The Federal Presence*, 280–335.
25. "Crowds Admire New Postoffice in Open House Program Sunday," *Tennessean*, November 19, 1934.
26. Ibid.
27. Ibid.
28. James Draeger, "The Art Deco Architecture of Nashville Architects Marr and Holman," Master's thesis, Middle Tennessee State University, 1986, 4.
29. Craig et al., *The Federal Presence*, 8, 14.
30. Bruns, *Great American Post Offices*, 81.
31. Draeger, "Art Deco Architecture," 83.
32. Alan Gowans, *Images of American Living: Four Centuries of Architecture and Furniture as Cultural Expression* (New York: Harper and Row, 1964), 441.
33. Alastair Duncan, *American Art Deco* (New York: Harry N. Abrams, 1986), 7–39.
34. U.S. Postal Service, *History of the United States Postal Service*, 8–14.
35. Marvin Runyon, interview by Christine Kreyling, July 6, 2000.
36. James Logan Howard, "History of Marr & Holman, Architects, Nashville, Tennessee," talk delivered to the Friends of the Nashville Room of the Nashville Public Library,

"Paragraphs of Nashville History," January 10, 1983. Manuscript, Creighton Collection, Metro Nashville Archives.
37. Ibid., 4.
38. Draeger, "Art Deco Architecture," and Howard, "History of Marr & Holman," among others, give 1910. Mrs. J. B. Chandler, "Thomas Scott Marr," *Silent Worker*, June 1929, 182–85, and the National Register Nomination, citing Joseph Herndon, "Architects in Tennessee until 1930, a Biographical Dictionary," Master's thesis, Columbia University, 1975, give 1913 and ca. 1913, respectively.
39. Howard, "History of Marr & Holman," 12.
40. Ibid., 5.
41. Joseph Holman to Joseph W. Byrns, TL (copy), October 31, 1913, Marr & Holman Collection.
42. Holman to Byrns, TL (copy), November 6, 1913, Marr & Holman Collection.
43. Holman to Byrns, TL (copy), July 13, 1915, Marr & Holman Collection.
44. Byrns to Holman, TLS, July 24, 1915, Marr & Holman Collection.
45. Howard, "History of Marr & Holman," 36, 26.
46. Ibid., 17.
47. Holman to Thomas Marr, TL (copy), July 13, 1917, Marr & Holman Collection.
48. Howard, "History of Marr & Holman," 11.
49. Ibid., 6.
50. Ibid., 10.
51. Ibid., 30.
52. Craig et al., *The Federal Presence*, 327.
53. Draeger, "Art Deco Architecture," 77.
54. "Messer to Make Trip to Nashville," *Nashville Banner*, May 19, 1933, 1.
55. Record Group 121, National Archives, Washington, D.C.
56. Howard, "History of Marr & Holman," 12.
57. Ibid., 4.
58. Ibid., 19.
59. Metro Nashville Historical Commission, "National Register of Historic Places Nomination: United States Post Office," Nashville, Tenn., 1984, photocopy, item 8, 1.
60. U.S. Postal Service, *History of the United States Postal Service*, 6.

BIBLIOGRAPHY

61. Pollye Braswell, "Nashville Invited to See New Million-Dollar Postoffice," *Tennessean Magazine*, November 18, 1934, 8–9.
62. Ibid.
63. Ibid.
64. Unless otherwise indicated, information in this section is from U.S. Postal Service, *History of the United States Postal Service*.
65. Bruns, *Great American Post Offices*, 21.
66. U.S. Postal Service, *History of the United States Postal Service*, 7.
67. U.S. Postal Service, *Nashville Division Update*, February–March 1989, 6–7.
68. Braswell, "Nashville Invited to See New Million-Dollar Postoffice," 8–9.
69. Quoted in Bruns, *Great American Post Offices*, 100.
70. Juanita Threalkill Johnson, interview by Christine Kreyling, April 6, 2000.
71. Bill Hudgins, "Post Office Awaits Final Holiday Rush," *Nashville Banner*, December 3, 1986.
72. Adell Crowe, "Nashville Firm to Design New Post Office Facility," *Tennessean*, December 31, 1982, 1–2.
73. Marvin Runyon, interview by Christine Kreyling, July 6, 2000.
74. Kathleen Gallagher, "Redevelopment Design Sought for Downtown Post Office," *Nashville Banner*, June 21, 1988.
75. Mary Hance, "Post Office Design Offered," *Nashville Banner*, January 21, 1989.

Ackerman, James. "Listening to Architecture." *Harvard Educational Review* 39, no. 4 (1969).
Andrews, Wayne. *Architecture, Ambition, and Americans: A History of American Architecture.* New York: The Free Press, 1964.
Beasely, Kay. "Hub of Wartime Transportation." *Nashville Banner*, October 15, 1986.
Betts, Benjamin F. "Is the Government Treating Architects Fairly?" *American Architect*, February 1931.
———. "The Government Should Get out of the Architectural Business." *American Architect*, May 1931.
"Big Building Year for City." *Nashville Banner*, December 29, 1929, 1.
Braswell, Pollye. "Nashville Invited to See New Million-Dollar Postoffice." *Tennessean Magazine*, November 18, 1934, 8–9.
Bruce, Edward, and Forbes Watson. *Art in Federal Buildings: An Illustrated History of the Treasury Department's New Program in Painting and Sculpture.* Washington, D.C.: Art in Federal Buildings, 1936.
Bruns, James H. *Great American Post Offices.* New York: John Wiley & Sons, 1998.
Bush, Donald J. *The Streamlined Decade.* New York: George Braziller, 1975.
Chandler, Mrs. J. B. "Thomas Scott Marr, Architect." *Silent Worker*, June 1929, 182–85.
Craig, Lois, et al. *The Federal Presence: Architecture, Politics, and Symbols in United States Government Building.* Cambridge, Mass.: MIT Press, 1978.
Cret, Paul P. "Ten Years of Modernism." *Federal Architect*, July 1933.
"Crowds Admire New Postoffice in Open House Program Sunday." *Tennessean*, November 19, 1934.
Crowe, Adell. "Nashville Firm to Design New Post Office Facility." *Tennessean*, December 31, 1982.
Cullinan, Peter. *The Post Office Department.* Washington, D.C.: Praeger Library of U.S. Government Departments and Agencies, 1968.
Doyle, Don H. *Nashville since the 1920s.* Knoxville: University of Tennessee Press, 1985.
Draeger, James. "The Art Deco Architecture of Nashville Architects Marr and Holman." Master's thesis, Middle Tennessee State University, 1986.

Duncan, Alastair. *American Art Deco.* New York: Harry N. Abrams, 1986.
Eberghard, Ernest. "Fifty Years of Agitation . . . for Better Design of Government Buidings and Government Employment of Private Architects." *American Architect*, June 1931.
Federal Architect 1, no. 1–11, no. 1 (July 1930–July 1940).
Fuller, Wayne E. *The American Mail: Enlarger of the Common Life.* Chicago: University of Chicago Press, 1972.
Gallagher, Kathleen. "Redevelopment Design Sought for Downtown Post Office." *Nashville Banner*, June 21, 1988.
Garver, Thomas H., ed. *Just before the War: Urban America from 1935 to 1941 as Seen by Photographers of the Farm Security Administration.* Exh. cat. Balboa, Calif.: Newport Harbor Art Museum, 1968.
German Library of Information. *A Nation Builds: Contemporary German Architecture.* New York: German Library of Information, 1940.
Gowans, Alan. *Images of American Living: Four Centuries of Architecture and Furniture as Cultural Expression.* New York: Harper and Row, 1964.
Hance, Mary, "Post Office Design Offered." *Nashville Banner*, January 21, 1989.
Heath, Ferry K. "The Federal Building Program." *Architectural Forum*, September 1931.
Hitchcock, Henry-Russell, and Philip Johnson. *The International Style.* New York: W. W. Norton & Company, 1966.
Howard, James Logan. "History of Marr & Holman, Architects, Nashville, Tennessee." Talk delivered to the Friends of the Nashville Room of the Nashville Public Library, "Paragraphs of Nashville History," January 10, 1983. Manuscript, Creighton Collection, Metro Nashville Archives.
Hudgins, Bill. "Post Office Awaits Final Holiday Rush." *Nashville Banner*, December 3, 1986.
Hurley, Jack F. *Portrait of a Decade: Roy Stryker and the Development of Documentary Photography in the Thirties.* Baton Rouge: Louisiana State University Press, 1972. Reprint. New York: Da Capo Press, 1977.
Kelly, Clyde. *United States Postal Policy.* New York: D. Appleton & Co., 1931.

Knowles, Susan. "A. C. Webb: Artist/Architect." Master's thesis, Vanderbilt University, 1986.

Kreyling, Christine, et al. *Classical Nashville: Athens of the South.* Nashville, Tenn.: Vanderbilt University Press, 1996.

Lee, Antoinette. *Architects to the Nation: The Rise and Decline of the Supervising Architect's Office.* New York: Oxford University Press, 2000.

L'Orange, H. P. *Art Forms and Civic Life in the Late Roman Empire.* Princeton, N.J.: Princeton University Press, 1965.

Marr & Holman Collection. Tennessee Historical Society Collection, Tennessee State Library & Archives, Nashville.

"Messer to Make Trip to Nashville." *Nashville Banner,* May 19, 1933, 1.

Metro Nashville Historical Commission. "National Register of Historic Places Nomination: United States Post Office." Nashville, Tenn., 1984. Photocopy.

Nashville's Agenda. *Twenty-one Goals for the Twenty-first Century.* Nashville, Tenn., January 1994.

———. *Action on Nashville's Agenda.* Nashville, Tenn., November 1994.

National Resources Committee. *Our Cities: Their Role in the National Economy.* Washington, D.C.: National Resources Committee, 1937.

Naylor, T. W., and E. R. Martin. *Nashville, Tennessee: Investigation in the Formulation of a Public Buildings' Program,* case no. 176,031-C, Treasury Department Papers, Record Group 121, National Archives, Washington, D.C.

New, Harry S. *United States Official Postal Guide,* 4th ser., 5, no. 3, monthly supplement. Washington, D.C.: Post Office Department, September 1925.

Park, Marlene, and Gerald E. Markowitz. *Democratic Vistas: Post Offices and Public Art in the New Deal.* Philadelphia: Temple University Press, 1984.

Patrick, James. *Architecture in Tennessee, 1768–1897.* Knoxville: University of Tennessee Press, 1981. Reprint. 1990.

Public Works Administration. *America Builds: The Record of PWA.* Washington, D.C.: Government Printing Office, 1939.

"Publix Theater Officials Here." *Nashville Banner,* October 23, 1930, 1.

Reynolds, Ann Vines. "Nashville's Custom House." *Tennessee Historical Quarterly* 37, no. 3 (fall 1978): 263–77.

Rodman, Selden. *Portrait of the Artist as an American: Ben Shahn: A Biography with Pictures.* New York: Harper and Brothers, 1951.

Scheele, Carl H. *Neither Snow nor Rain . . . The Story of the United States Mails.* Washington, D.C.: Smithsonian Institution Press, 1970.

Scheele, Carl H. *A Short History of the Mail Service.* Washington, D.C.: Smithsonian Institution Press, 1970.

Short, C. W., and R. Stanley Brown. *Public Buildings: A Survey of Architecture of Projects Constructed by Federal and Other Governmental Bodies between the Years 1933 and 1939.* Washington, D.C.: U.S. Government Printing Office, 1939.

Stryker, Roy E. "Documentary Photography." *Complete Photographer,* April 1942. In Jack F. Hurley, *Portrait of a Decade: Roy Stryker and the Development of Documentary Photography in the Thirties.* Baton Rouge: Louisiana State University Press, 1972. Reprint. New York: Da Capo Press, 1977.

Summerfield, Arthur E. *U.S. Mail: The Story of the United States Postal Service.* New York: Holt, Rinehart & Winston, 1960.

Tierney, John T. *Postal Reorganization: Managing the Public's Business.* Boston: Auburn House Publishing Company, 1981.

U.S. Department of the Treasury. *A History of Public Buildings: Under the Control of the Treasury Department.* Washington, D.C.: Government Printing Office, 1901.

U.S. Department of the Treasury, Supervising Architect's Office. *Annual Report.* Washington, D.C., 1933–34.

U.S. Postal Service. *History of the United States Postal Service, 1775–1993.* Washington, D.C.: U.S. Postal Service, 1993.

Work Projects Administration for the State of Tennessee, Federal Writers Project. *The WPA Guide to Tennessee.* New York: Viking Press, 1939. Reprint. Knoxville: University of Tennessee Press, 1986.

White, Theodore B. *Paul Philippe Cret, Architect and Teacher.* Philadelphia: Art Alliance Press, 1973.

Wilson, Richard Guy, Dianne H. Pilgrim, and Dickran Tashjian. *The Machine Age in America, 1918–1941.* Exh. cat. New York: The Brooklyn Museum, 1986.